ECHO OF EDEN

HOW YOUR IDENTITY IMPACTS YOUR MARRIAGE

TYLER OLSEN, LMHC

FOREWORD BY
DR. LES HARDIN

In Loving Memory of Kyle Olsen
Your story is written into every page of this book.
I miss you.

CONTENTS

THE SHAPE OF IDENTITY AND THE STRAIN OF CONFLICT

Dr. Les Hardin
Professor of New Testament
Kentucky Christian University

THESEUS AND BATMAN

In his *Parallel Lives* Plutarch tells a story about Theseus, the mythical founder of Athens. After slaying the minotaur, Theseus rescued the children of Athens from King Minos, put them on a boat, and sailed them away to Delos. Each year the citizens of Athens commemorated the journey by sailing the Ship of Theseus from Athens to Delos. After 500 years of reenactments, the ship naturally needed repairing. Broken oars needed to be replaced. Torn sails needed mending. Rotting boards required replacement. The question Plutarch poses is this: After 500 years of replacements, is it still the Ship of Theseus?

> "They took away the old timbers from time
> to time, and put new and sound ones in

their places, so that the vessel became a
standing illustration for the philosophers
in the mooted question of growth, some
declaring that it remained the same,
others that it was not the same vessel."

(PLUTARCH, *LIFE OF THESEUS*, 23.1)

What exactly is the Ship of Theseus? Is it the material
form, the actual boat that carried the children away from
King Minos? Or is the exact form of the ship inconsequential
to the idea it manifests? Or this: Is the *identity* of the Ship of
Theseus tied to its *material form*? Or is its identity and
consciousness *separate* from the wood, sails, and oars?

Identity questions permeate the Batman saga. From a
meta critical, behind-the-fourth-wall perspective, who is
Batman? Is it Adam West? Michael Keaton? Val Kilmer?
Christian Bale? Ben Affleck? George Clooney? Robert Pattin-
son? When I say "Batman," whose face comes to mind?

But immerse yourself in the storyline and more identity
questions begin to surface. Is Batman a role specifically
limited to and only executable by Bruce Wayne? Or, ala
"Codename V" (in Alan Moore's *V for Vendetta*), can anyone
become the Batman? Can anyone don the mask and cape
and fight crime? Or does this role *only* emerge from the
trauma of Bruce Wayne seeing his parents gunned down in
an alley behind the theater? Without that trauma, is there
such a person as Batman? Is Batman's legacy attainable
without Bruce Wayne's fortune? All the things he uses to
fight crime are funded by his (and his father's) fortunes. A
pauper would have trouble taking on this role.

And this final question: Is Bruce Wayne moonlighting as

Batman? Or has Batman emerged as the true identity, masquerading by day as Bruce Wayne?

These are all questions about identity. And the issue of identity is crucial to what you're about to read in this book.

WHAT IS IDENTITY?

What do we mean when we say "identity"? What does that term refer to? I taught a graduate course in a spiritual formation program a few years ago, one that focused on how identity shapes your spiritual growth (and how your growth shapes your identity), and in prepping for the course, I began looking for a standard definition of identity. The literature is vast, and you can rest easy that I have no intention of reciting it here. But here's the takeaway: *There is no standard definition of identity.*

Most of the literature defines identity (in layman's terms) as "Who I am"—my temperament, desires, fears, likes, dislikes, attitudes, experiences, and the way I see the world. But, like the Ship of Theseus, who I am is ever-changing. I used to be a son, and I still am. But at some point, I became a father, and then a grandfather. I used to be single, then I was married. And I'm more mature than I was at 18. "Who I am" is not "who I was."

Some of the literature includes in the definition of identity an awareness of "What I do." In many circles the term for this is "vocation" (which is broader than any job I have at the moment). It's the sense that (well, let's let BatWayne chime in here), "It's not who I am but what I *do* that defines me." I am a Bible teacher, specializing in discipleship and high-level Bible teaching. But that vocation has expressed itself as pastor, youth pastor, education minister, elder, and professor in a variety of contexts. The role and identity of professor involves certain actions: daily reading, writing, research, designing syllabi and course notes, administration of learning management software, participating in faculty and department meetings, preaching and teaching in churches on the weekends, and promoting the university's endeavors. Who I am is significantly shaped by what I do.

"Who I am" and "what I do" are just definitions, though. Where does my identity come from? Is my identity **fixed**, given at birth and imbued in my consciousness? The personality profiles that began with the philosopher Galen, reworked by Carl Jung, Isabel Briggs Myers and Katherine Cook Briggs, and now find expression in tools like the Enneagram are attempting to categorize latent tendencies, patterns, problems, and motivations prevalent in each of us at the deepest levels. Or is my identity **fluid**, changing and morphing as my life enters new eras, situations, and experiences? Is identity **forged**? Or is it **innate**? How much of my identity is **somatic**, tied to my bodily experience? A healthy athlete has a body-identity just as an amputee does. Several folks in Scripture are known by their somatic identity: Simon the Leper, Blind Bartimaeus, Zaccheus, and Mephibosheth.

For the Christian, the identity questions become more intricate and involved because of the indwelling presence and gifting of the Holy Spirit. "To each one is given the manifestation of the Spirit for the common good" (1 Cor. 12:7). How does the indwelling of the Spirit shape my identity? Every part of the New Testament suggests that life in Christ brings good and lasting change—a shift in identity. What role does the sanctification process (i.e. the process of becoming more Christlike) play in a Christian's identity?

And here's a question that weirded out my graduate students (and on which I couldn't get much discussion): what role does sin play in the shaping of a Christian identity? Paul was redeemed from his murderous, hate-filled religious life. But there's not a single time in his letters that, recounting his redemption, he doesn't remind his readers (and himself) who he used to be. "Christ Jesus came into the world to save sinners, of whom I am the worst" (1 Tim. 1:15). He's not just Paul the Apostle. He's Paul the Used-to-be-a-Zealot. His past sinful life shaped his present Christian identity.

IDENTITY AND CONFLICT

These questions about identity—where it comes from, how it develops, and whether it's escapable—are difficult. And what I've mentioned so far is only the surface-level, the part of the iceberg barely visible above the water.

Those wrestling with identity and trying to provide a clear definition of it all agree that there's also a *social* component to who we are. Identity is both personal and social. Say "identity" and our minds tend to gravitate toward the personal aspects. But in very real ways my identity is shaped by the family I was raised in, the community I spend time in, the people I went to high school and college with, the people I work with, those I worship with, my in-laws, and my children and grandchildren. And their identities (individual and corporate) are shaped in significant ways by my presence among them.

In every social context there are problems. Conflicts. Arguments. Disagreements. Offenses. Navigating those interpersonal conflicts has just as much to do with identity as it does with maturity. When involved in a conflict, does your temperament (that part of your identity that is innate and persistent) prefer to go away and think about things, mull over what you need to do and then later come back to the conversation? Or does your temperament as an external processor require a discussion about the issues in that very moment? Does your identity (through whatever childhood and family trauma might have occurred) make you see every disagreement as *combat,* activating a primal response to *win*? Or in those moments do you seek peace and reconciliation, even if that means submerging your own hurts and desires?

Navigating the identity issues that arise in interpersonal conflicts is the focus of this book. Our responses in conflict situations are often dictated by deep-seated identity issues. "I'm afraid my partner is going to leave me." "She only brought this up because she thinks I don't provide enough." "His comment is a veiled way of saying he doesn't find me attractive anymore." "She doesn't respect me." "He doesn't love me." When words hurt, and the emotions kick in, it sometimes becomes very hard to listen to what the other person is *actually saying. Listening* takes a back seat to *insecurity* and we fail to truly communicate.

This book will help you navigate all that. In the following pages, Tyler demonstrates how strains in our relationships often originate in deep-seated insecurities and identity issues. One of the keys to navigating interpersonal conflicts is to draw on the resources available to us from the Word and the Spirit. In other words, Tyler will help you understand that relationship stress is often centered in deep-rooted identity issues, and then will help you find the truthfulness of your identity in Christ as a way of navigating them toward reconciliation and peace. The truth that you are loved by God (Rom. 5:8, 1 John 4:10), seated in the heavenlies with Christ (Eph 2:6), and adopted into the family as God's child (Eph. 1:5, 1 John 3:1). The truth that you are a sinner (Rom. 3:23), that you're imperfect and unrighteous (Rom. 3:10), and that even the best of us find ourselves in interpersonal conflict (Gal. 2:11-14). The truth that the former provides the resources you need to adjudicate the latter and lead you to peace in your relationships.

INTRODUCTION

While writing my first book, *The Art of Apologizing,* I realized something deeper was at play in nearly every conflict I explored, identity. Before we can embrace forgiveness, we have to know who we are. We were created by God with intentionality and purpose, and the more we understand the Creator, the more we understand ourselves. That truth has everything to do with how we love, how we handle conflict, and how we heal in marriage.

This book builds on the foundation of my earlier work, but with a sharper focus: how embracing your God-given identity changes the way you show up in your marriage. Through practical tools, real-life reflections, and biblical insights, we'll explore what it means to love not from insecurity or control, but from wholeness in Christ.

This book is written for Christian couples committed to growing in their marriage, and particularly for those walking through seasons of conflict, distance, or insecurity. It's not intended to address abusive relationships, divorce recovery, or singleness, though the truths of identity may still resonate in those journeys as well.

Scripture and prayer aren't just spiritual accessories in this journey, they're essential. They don't just guide us; they ground us. And the truth at the heart of this book is this: marriage is a reflection of God's love, not because we've figured it out, but because He's still working in us.

Jesus modeled sacrificial love. He led with grace. He stayed faithful, even when others pulled away. That's the kind of love we're called to mirror. But let me be clear, you are not the Holy Spirit for your spouse. Your job isn't to fix them, change them, or highlight their every flaw. That kind of pressure not only builds resentment; it can drive your spouse further from God.

So don't read this book with your spouse's faults in mind. Don't highlight passages hoping they'll "get the hint." Don't be the one saying "Amen" during a sermon when it's their issue being addressed. That's not love. That's passive-aggression in spiritual clothing.

Instead, be a conduit of Christ's love. Let what God pours into you overflow into your marriage. Encourage. Pray. Be patient. Stay humble. As we move forward, I'll ask you to take an honest look at your own role in your relationship, just like I'm doing in mine. This won't be easy. It will stretch you. But I'm walking this road with you, not ahead of you. This isn't just a message for your spouse. It's for you. It's for me. My hope is that every page of this book challenges me first, to grow, to lead with love, to become more like Christ in my own marriage. You're not doing this alone. The Holy Spirit is working. Let's posture ourselves to receive that work, apply it, and grow together.

1

REDISCOVERING TRUE IDENTITY

THERE ONCE WAS A BOY, just an ordinary kid in the grand scheme of things. He wasn't anyone special or at least that's what he believed. His days were filled with chores, the kind of menial tasks that make you feel invisible. He wasn't born into nobility. He didn't have a family name that carried weight. He was just a nobody, a face in the crowd. At least, that's what the world told him. And eventually, he started to believe it too.

But somewhere deep beneath the surface, there was always this gnawing sense that there had to be more. He couldn't explain it, and he wasn't sure he wanted to. It was easier to keep his head down and stay unnoticed. Better to survive quietly than to risk stepping out and fail. He crafted a mindset where avoiding risk was wisdom. That smallness was safety.

Then came the day that shattered everything he thought he knew about himself. The town square was alive with excitement. A strange contest had captured everyone's attention. In the middle of the square stood a sword buried deep in a stone. The proclamation was clear: "Whoever pulls this sword from the stone shall be king."

The strongest men in the land lined up, confident that the sword and the crown belonged to them. One by one, they failed. The crowd jeered and whispered, turning the whole thing into a spectacle. It was absurd. Everyone knew kings weren't made by pulling swords from stones. Kings came from bloodlines, battles, and power, not contests. Yet, people still tried.

The boy was there, watching from the sidelines. He had no business stepping forward. He wasn't strong. He wasn't important. He wasn't... anything. But life has a way of dragging us into moments we don't feel ready for.

Before he knew it, he was standing in front of the sword. He reached out, and wrapped his hands around the hilt. And then something happened, not to the sword, to him. The sword didn't respond to strength or effort. It responded to identity. The boy wasn't *becoming* someone in that moment. He *already* was someone. The act of pulling the sword didn't make him the rightful king, it revealed it. His identity as king wasn't born in that square; it had been there all along, hidden beneath years of doubt and obscurity.

When the sword slid free, the crowd erupted. Shock. Awe. Disbelief. This boy, this nobody, now stood holding the symbol of kingship. But for the boy, the moment wasn't triumph. It was terror. The sword felt heavier than anything he'd ever held. Not because of its weight, but because of what it meant. He wasn't just holding a weapon, he was holding responsibility, destiny, and identity. And that terrified him.

You see, the sword didn't give him value. It didn't make him worthy. It simply exposed what had always been true.

But stepping into that truth wasn't easy. He doubted himself. He shrunk back under the weight of it all. He faltered. He even tried to disappear back into the shadows again. Yet every time he did, something inside him kept whispering: "You are more than this."

The boy, as you might have guessed by now, was Arthur. Yes, *that* Arthur. King Arthur. And while the sword in the stone might be the most famous part of his story, it's not the most important. The real story isn't about pulling a sword. It's about the identity that had always been his. The sword was just a moment of clarity in a world trying to tell him he wasn't enough.

Arthur's story is ours. We, too, live in a world that tells us that our identity is tied to what we do, what we achieve, what we fail to become, or what others say about us. But identity doesn't start with accomplishment. It starts with creation. You weren't made valuable because of what you've done. You were made valuable because of who made you. Your true identity is already there. Unshakable, purposeful, and waiting to be uncovered. The sword doesn't make you who you are, it only reveals who you've always been.

When we live outside of our true identity, when we chase false versions of ourselves, we find nothing but insecurity and inconsistency. We live in fear, constantly trying to prove our worth to a world that will never be satisfied.

False identity always comes with a cost: instability in your behavior and insecurity in your value. But when you embrace who you truly are, who you've been all along, you begin to walk in strength, clarity, and security. You stop chasing validation and start living from a place of security.

Arthur's journey wasn't about becoming someone new.

It was about becoming someone honest. It was about stepping into who he had always been. And ours is no different.

The question isn't "Am I enough?"

It's "Am I willing to claim the identity that's been mine
all along?"

THE SHIP AND THE SOUL

In the foreword, Dr. Hardin asked whether the Ship of
Theseus is still the same ship after every board, rope, and
sail has been replaced over time. Philosophers have debated
that question for centuries. This shows how identity is often
seen as something that shifts over time. Piece by piece, it's
shaped by new experiences and seasons of life. And in one
sense, that's true: our roles change, our perspectives deepen,
our circumstances leave their mark. It's true that I am not
exactly the same today as I was 10 years ago. And my
marriage isn't the same today as it was on our wedding day.
My perspectives have shifted over the years.

But here's where I want to be clear: your true identity,
the one God spoke over you before you could earn it or ruin
it, is not up for revision. In Christ, you are secure, chosen,
and unshakably loved. That part doesn't change.

What does change is our relationship to that truth.
Sometimes we move toward it, anchoring deeper into who
God says we are. Other times we drift from it, living as if our
worth depends on performance, control, or approval. The
Ship of Theseus reminds us that slow change is inevitable.
The question is, are the "boards" being replaced in you
drawing you closer to the truth of your identity, or further
into the fog of insecurity?

That's where Arthur's story fits. His sword-in-the-stone

moment wasn't the day he became worthy, it was the day he stopped pretending he wasn't. And in the same way our journey is both a decisive awakening to our identity and a daily choice to realign with it.

THE SLOW DRIFT FROM TRUTH

Arthur's story shows how stepping into your true identity is a decisive moment, a sword out of the stone kind of awakening. But the Ship of Theseus reminds us that identity isn't just revealed in a single moment, it's shaped, sometimes strengthened, sometimes distorted, over time. One shows the spark, the other shows the slow burn.

In my own life, I've experienced both. There have been moments when I felt God pulling me back into the truth of who I am, like Arthur gripping the sword. And there have been seasons where, piece by piece, I drifted without realizing it, like a ship being rebuilt with boards that didn't quite fit the original design. I've wandered off the path of who I really am, not knowing how I got there, and not knowing how to get back. But even then, something inside me said, *This isn't it. This isn't who you are.*

When we fall off the path of our true identity we start to second-guess our worth. We question whether we are lovable, capable, or even wanted. That insecurity shows up in different ways: sometimes as defensiveness, sometimes as withdrawal. Sometimes it's passive; other times, controlling. But it always pulls us further from who we are meant to be.

This instability doesn't just affect us. It bleeds into our marriage, friendships, and even our relationship with God. We start building walls to protect the fragile, false version of ourselves. We stop showing up. We stop trusting. We stop leaning into grace.

But here's the truth: the further we stray from who we are in Christ, the more we disconnect from the peace, strength, clarity, and consistency He offers. That's why reclaiming our identity is never about striving, it's about surrender. It's about shedding the false stories we've believed and stepping boldly into the unshakeable truth of who we are. When we realign with who we are in Christ, we don't just find our own strength, we find the capacity to bring consistency, intimacy, and love into every relationship, especially our marriage.

FINDING YOUR WAY BACK

When you live in a false identity, it's as if you've wandered off the path you were meant to walk. At some point, the lies we've believed, the wounds we've carried, and the false narratives we've absorbed detour us into the treacherous, uncharted forest of a false identity.

Each painful experience, each unchallenged belief, leads us further off course, deeper into the woods, away from the clarity and peace of who we were created to be. In this forest, the trees are thick with insecurity. The shadows stretch long with doubt. It's easy to feel disoriented and alone, stumbling over roots of past trauma and getting tangled in the vines of comparison, fear and shame.

I've been in this forest. For me, it wasn't obvious at first. Somewhere along the way, I started tying my worth to how happy my wife was, not just with me, but with her life. If she was content, I felt like I was doing okay. But if she was discouraged or upset, I took it personally. I didn't realize it at the time, but I had begun measuring my identity by how well I could keep things "good" at home. That pressure built quietly over time. Eventually, I found myself exhausted and honestly resentful of her emotional state. That's when I realized I had drifted. Not in my love for her, but in my understanding of who I was.

Some wounds are massive, like childhood abuse, betrayal, or abandonment. Others are subtle, like a parent's unmet expectations, being overlooked, or not getting picked on the playground. But whether loud or quiet, those wounds plant seeds that lure us off the path of our true identity. We were never meant to stay lost here.

So, how do we find our way back? Like any journey, we need two essential pieces of information: we need to know where we are (our false identity) and where we're going (our true identity). If we don't recognize the lies we've believed and if we don't get honest about the false self we've been living from, we will keep circling the woods, mistaking motion for progress. We'll hustle. Perform. Prove. But it won't bring peace. **False identity always leads to fear-based performance. True identity leads to freedom-based purpose.**

Reclaiming your true identity means tracing your way back, pinpointing the lies that have detoured you and reorienting your heart toward the unshakable truth of who you were made to be. It's not just about moving forward, it's about moving with clarity, back to the road you were always meant to walk.

WHO ARE YOU?

When I meet with clients who may be really struggling with a false identity, one of the first and most important questions I ask is, "Who are you?" It seems simple. But for many, it's one of the hardest questions to answer. How would you answer that question?

Most people start by talking about what they do, their job, their role as a parent, spouse, or friend. But those things, while meaningful, don't define who you are. There's a big difference between what you *do* and *who you are*.

You are not what you've done. You are not what's been done to you. You are who God created you to be. And that truth starts at the very beginning, before performance, before failure, before fear had a chance to whisper lies into your heart.

You were made in the image of God. And God is love.

That means your capacity to be loved is not something you earn, it's something you are. Built into your design. Stamped into your soul. You are lovable because of your Creator, not your behavior.

And here's the unshakable part: nothing you've done, nothing you've failed to do, and nothing you've suffered can undo the image you were made in. You might forget it. You might bury it. But it's still there, waiting to be reclaimed. You can't ruin what God has already declared good. You can't outrun the love you were made for.

Your identity is not determined by your title, your achievements, or even your failures. Think about it like DNA, your behavior doesn't change your DNA, your actions don't rewrite the truth of who you were created to be.

When I push my clients to dig deeper, many realize they

don't actually know who they are at the core. That realization can be both unsettling and enlightening. It's unsettling because it reveals how often we've built our identity on shifting ground: careers, relationships, or accomplishments. But it's liberating because it cracks open the door to something deeper. Something eternal.

I'll be honest, I never really spent much time asking myself, *"Who am I?"* It always felt a little abstract. I was more focused on doing the next right thing, being who I needed to be for the people around me. But looking back, I can see how my identity was constantly being shaped by whatever was going on around me: circumstances, relationships, or expectations. I didn't realize it, but I was picking up pieces from each role I played and calling that "me." I didn't have a solid foundation. My identity wasn't something I saw as fundamentally set by my Creator. It was something I thought I had to keep earning, proving, or maintaining. And that left me unsteady, even when life on the outside looked fine.

When you anchor yourself in God's truth, not your performance, not the expectations of others, you begin to live with authenticity and security. That shift from false identity to true identity in Christ doesn't just change how you see yourself. It doesn't just adjust your self-perception. It transforms your relationships. Especially your marriage.

MADE IN HIS IMAGE: THE SIGNATURE OF GOD

In the beginning, God knelt down into the dust and created man, *Adam,* which comes from the Hebrew *adamah,* meaning earth or dirt. He was formed in the hands of God out of nothing more than lifeless clay. But then God leaned in and with a single breath, the *ruaḥ*, the Spirit of life, filled the lungs of Adam. Blood stirred, and the heart beat for the first time. Adam opened his eyes and the very first thing he saw was the face of his Creator. His first inhale was God's exhale. His first awareness was not of the world, but of the One who made it. His first identity was not worker, not husband, not even "man", it was *image-bearer*, face-to-face with God.

That is where identity begins. Not in performance. Not in relationships. Not in the stories we tell ourselves. Identity begins in the dirt touched by divine breath. Every cell, every thought, every heartbeat echoes that moment. You were made to carry God's image into the world.

And when we forget this, when we drift from it, we don't just lose our sense of self, we lose the security that only comes from knowing who breathed life into us.

When Genesis declares that humanity was made in the *image of God* (*tselem Elohim*), it's not giving us a metaphor to feel better about ourselves. It's revealing a profound truth: you were created with intention. Your identity is not a social accident or a psychological construct. It's divinely designed.

But what does that mean? And how can we grasp it in a world that often measures identity by performance, popularity, or productivity? One way is to pay attention to how God has woven his signature into creation itself, in biology, in our brains, in language, and in the way we experience emotion. Science doesn't replace Scripture, however it often provides a surprising echo of it. Together, they can awaken us to the reality that we were never meant to wonder if we mattered.

———

The Body That Bears Witness

Science tells us that emotional tears, the kind we cry in grief or joy, are chemically different from reflex tears (like when dust gets in your eye). Emotional tears carry stress hormones and natural painkillers that don't appear in reflex tears (Frey, 1985; Vingerhoets, 2013). In other words, your body was designed with a way to process sorrow and release stress. God didn't just make us to feel; he made us to heal through feeling.

Or take oxytocin, the hormone released through touch, affection, and even shared eye contact. Neuroscientists call it the "bonding hormone" because it literally wires us to trust and connect. What theologians have always said, "it is not good for man to be alone", is written into our cells. The very architecture of your body testifies that you were created for love, safety, and connection.

Even your nervous system tells the story. The vagus nerve, the largest cranial nerve in your body, helps regulate stress and social engagement. When you slow your breathing or hear a calm voice, the vagus nerve signals safety to your body. Fear eases, defenses lower, and you become available for relationship. The body was designed for intimacy long before psychology gave us language for it.

The Brain That Can Be Renewed

Scripture says, *"Be transformed by the renewing of your mind"* (Romans 12:2). For centuries that sounded purely spiritual, but neuroscience now confirms it's also literal. Your brain has neuroplasticity, the capacity to rewire itself through repeated thought and practice. Every time you meditate on Scripture, resist a false narrative, or lean into a new behavior of love, your brain builds new pathways. What Paul called "renewal" two millennia ago, neuroscientists now observe in brain scans (Lazar et al., 2005; Kober et al., 2017).

God hardwired change into you. That means your false identity isn't fixed. Fear doesn't have to write your story. Your brain can heal. And when it does, your marriage heals too.

The Cosmos That Reflects Its Maker

And since God works in ways far greater than we can understand, let's take a step back further. The same fractal patterns that govern rivers also shape blood vessels. The same spirals in galaxies appear in seashells and fingerprints. The Creator leaves patterns, like brushstrokes, across scales of existence, from the cosmic to the cellular. These repeating rhythms whisper: life was not random, it was patterned (Rees, 1999; Collins, 2009).

Identity is not found in chaos; it's revealed in design. And your life, too, has been patterned, not by accident, but by intention.

The Emotions That Preach

Even your emotional life tells the truth if you know how to listen. We talked about how grief changes the chemistry of your tears. Joy registers in the body's release of endorphins. But there's more, prayer lights up the brain in ways similar to being with someone you love. In other words, communion with God doesn't just "feel" real, your body participates in it.

This means your emotions are not accidents or interruptions to faith. They are signposts, telling you when you've wandered from truth or when you're resting in it. They remind you that you were made for intimacy, with God and with others.

The Signature of God

From the tears that heal, to the neurons that rewire, to the Hebrew words that name you, everything about your design points to a truth deeper than biology or psychology can reach: you are made in the image of God.

You are not random. You are not replaceable. You are not what you do. You are who He says you are.

And when you embrace that truth, you don't just find security within yourself. You bring stability, peace, and intimacy into your marriage. Because when you stop demanding your spouse to prove your worth, you can finally give love freely, the way you were designed to.

TRUE VS. FALSE IDENTITIES

As you explore who you really are, remember that your identity is unchanging because it's based on God's eternal truth. You are His beloved child, created with purpose and value that go beyond any earthly measure. You are not what the world says about you. You are not what your worst moment says about you. You are who God says you are.

"...you are fearfully and wonderfully made."

(Psalm 139:14) [1]
"His masterpiece, created for good works." (Ephesians 2:10)
"Chosen, loved, and redeemed." (Colossians
3:12, Romans 8:38-39)

These truths aren't suggestions. They are the foundation of your identity. And when you build on that foundation, your confidence, peace, and stability don't rise and fall with your circumstances. Here is the best news: even *you* can't mess this up. You don't have the authority to rewrite what God has already declared. The creation doesn't override the Creator.

Honestly though, living from that truth isn't easy. We live in a world that's constantly trying to redefine us. The number on a paycheck, the amount of followers, the attempt to be approved by others, all of it tries to author your identity. And if you're not grounded in God's truth, the noise can drown out His voice. That's why it's critical to be intentional. You have to anchor yourself, not in affirmation from others, but in the still, steady truth of who God says you are.

In marriage, this understanding becomes even more vital. When you don't know who you are, you will start looking to your spouse to fill in the gaps. To validate you. To settle your insecurities. To hold you up when you can't hold yourself together. And while healthy affirmation is a beautiful part of a marriage, your spouse was never meant to carry the burden of defining your worth. That's a weight only God can bear.

---

1.   See FAQ on page 165

Think about it this way: if your identity is tied to your job, what happens when you lose it? If it's tied to being a parent, who are you when your kids grow up and leave the house? If it's tied to your spouse's approval, what happens when conflict arises, or they let you down? These shifting identities lead to insecurity, which then spills into your marriage, creating tension and unmet expectations. False identities create fragile marriages. They led to disconnection, blame, and control.

But when your identity is rooted in Christ, you bring a secure, whole person into the relationship. You don't need your spouse to complete you. You're already complete in Him. That's the freedom to love without fear, to support each other without pressure, to serve each other without resentment. Wives, it frees you to live with respect and submission, not out of fear or inferiority, but out of confidence in who you are. Husbands, it frees you to love sacrificially, not to prove something, but because you've already been filled by the One who gave you everything.

So, let me ask you again: *Who are you?*

This isn't a rhetorical question. It's an invitation to dive deeper, to strip away the false identities you've adopted, and to reclaim the truth of who God created you to be.

- You are not what you've done.
- You are not what's been done to you.
- You are not what others expect.
- You are who God created you to be.

When you live from that identity, you don't just find peace within yourself, you bring peace into your marriage. And that changes *everything*.

And as we move forward, I want to be clear, I didn't come up with this list in a vacuum. These are the lies I've believed, sometimes silently, sometimes loud enough to shake my marriage. I didn't always know they were lies, they felt like truth because they were rooted in pain. But slowly, through counseling, reflection, and God's grace, I started to name them. And when I did, I started to break their power.

Here are the false identities I discovered in my own marriage:

1. If you're unhappy with me, I've failed.
→ *False identity: I'm a failure.*

We start to believe that someone else's emotions are a reflection of our worth. But failure doesn't define you. Mistakes make you human, *not unlovable.* True identity rests in knowing that your value is fixed, rooted in who you are, not in achieving perfection.

2. If your eyes wander, it's because I wasn't enough.
→ *False identity: I'm not enough.*

Their choices reflect their own struggle, not your value. Your worth isn't up for debate. You are fearfully and wonderfully made, period. Your worth is inherent and unchanging, not contingent on anyone else's choices. Your identity isn't found in comparison or competition. It's secure and complete, regardless of anyone's wandering gaze. No external validation or comparison can alter your true identity.

3. If you reject me, it means you don't really love me.
→ *False identity: I'm not lovable.*

Rejection wounds, but it doesn't rewrite your identity. You are loved, not because others say so, but because God declared it from the beginning. Love isn't measured by perfect moments of acceptance; it's found in commitment and grace through imperfection. You are lovable simply because you were created in love, and nothing can take that away.

4. If you criticize me, it's because you don't think I'm capable.
→ *False identity: I'm not capable.*

Critique isn't always an attack. Growth doesn't mean weakness. Your capability was given by God, not measured by feedback. Critique isn't a reflection of your capability. Your true identity as a capable and purposeful individual isn't diminished by feedback. God equips you for every good work, and your potential is not defined by the opinions of others.

5. If I open up, I'll burden you.
→ *False identity: I'm a burden.*

This lie keeps you silent. But you were created to connect. Vulnerability isn't a weight, it's a bridge. You are not a burden.

You're a partner. Your voice matters, and your feelings are worth being heard. Healthy relationships thrive on shared burdens, where love is shown by supporting one another. Your spouse is not meant to carry your emotions alone, but they are meant to walk beside you as you share life together.

6. I'm only as good as what I provide.
→ *False identity: My worth = my output.*

This performance mindset crushes intimacy. You matter not because of what you do or provide, but because of who you are. While contributing to your marriage and family is important, your identity is not defined by your output. True security in your identity allows you to provide freely, without the fear that your value depends on it.

7. If you want space, it means you want to leave.
→ *False identity: I'll be abandoned.*

Space doesn't mean rejection, it can be necessary for reflection and growth. You are never truly alone, and your worth doesn't depend on constant closeness. Trust that love remains even when physical or emotional space is needed.

8. If you don't appreciate me, it means you don't care.
→ *False identity: I don't matter.*

Appreciation feels good, but your worth isn't measured by praise. You are seen and known, even when your efforts go unnoticed. Your value isn't tied to praise or acknowledgment. You are valuable simply because of who you are, and your worth doesn't fluctuate with external affirmation.

Trust that your contributions matter, even when they go unseen.

WRAP UP

False identities are subtle. They take root quietly, often planted by wounds, rejection, comparison, or unmet expectations. But left unchallenged, they grow into distorted narratives that shape how we see ourselves, and how we relate to others.

That's why the first step to reclaiming your true identity is recognizing the lies. False identities thrive in the shadows. But when brought into light, they lose their power.

The next step is to replace them with truth. For every false identity, there is truth rooted in God's Word:

- "I'm a failure," the truth declares, "I am more than my mistakes."
- "I'm not enough," the truth boldly proclaims, "I am made in the image of God, complete and chosen."
- "I'm not lovable" turns into "Nothing can separate me from the love of Christ."

In marriage, when we operate from false identities, we create tension and disconnection. We put weight on our spouse to affirm, validate and fix what only God can. This creates a cycle of unmet expectations and disappointment, leaving both partners frustrated and disconnected.

But when we choose to live from our true identity, we bring security, peace, and strength into our relationship. We stop reaching for approval. Instead we stand firm in who we are.

Ask yourself:

1. What false identities have you unknowingly carried into your marriage?
2. Are there areas where you've tied your worth to your spouse's actions or emotions?

Every one of us has wandered off the path of our true identity and gotten lost in something false. Every one of us, except Jesus. He's the only one who never lived from a false identity. And that's why He's the only one who can restore ours. It's a continual journey, one that I am on too. There are days I drift, when old lies whisper, when fear creeps in, when I forget who I am. But I've learned not to stay there. I've learned to trace my way back to the truth. Not perfectly, but intentionally. Because when I live from that place, everything shifts, not just inside me, but in my marriage, my parenting, and my faith.

The journey to reclaim your true identity isn't easy, but it's worth it. For you. For your marriage. For the legacy you want to build. Because before you can fix what's broken between you and your spouse, you have to be honest about what's broken inside of you. Every one of us is either moving closer to the truth of our identity or further from it. There's no standing still. The closer you move toward it, the more your marriage becomes a place of safety, connection, and grace. Not because you or your spouse are perfect, but because you're anchored in the One who is.

———

Go Deeper With These Verses

Psalm 139:14, Ephesians 2:10, Colossians 3:12, Romans 8:38

———

APPLICATION

Your identity fluctuates between the truth and lies: what God says about you, and what the world (or past wounds) have falsely named you.

Spend time with these three prompts:

1. **Who or what has shaped how you see yourself?** List a few influential voices: parents, culture, failure, success, your spouse, your faith story.
2. **Which roles or labels have become part of your identity?** Think: "peacemaker," "failure," "provider," "too much," "not enough." Which of these are roles you've carried? Which ones have tried to define you?
3. **After reading Psalm 139:14, Ephesians 2:10, Colossians 3:12, and Romans 8:28, what words does God use to describe you?** Write those words down. Let them interrupt the false labels you've internalized.

This chapter isn't about changing behavior. It's about

rediscovering who you were *before* fear, shame, or pride started writing your story.

This week, return to those Scriptures each day. Read them slowly. Out loud. As if God is speaking directly to you, because He is.

———

Pray This:

Heavenly Father,

Thank You for creating me with purpose, value, and love. In a world that constantly tries to define me by my achievements, failures, and the opinions of others, I often lose sight of who I truly am. I confess that I have walked the path of false identities, believing lies that have left me feeling insecure, unworthy, and disconnected from You and the people I love. I recognize that the more I wander away from You, the more my life is filled with sin.

Lord, I ask for Your guidance as I seek to rediscover my true identity. Reveal the areas where I've placed my worth in things that cannot sustain me. Help me to recognize the false identities I've clung to and replace them with the unshakable truth of who You say I am.

Teach me to stand firm in the knowledge that I am fearfully and wonderfully made, Your beloved child, chosen and redeemed. Let this truth bring peace to my heart, clarity to my mind, and strength to my relationships. Help me to reflect Your love and grace in all that I do, especially within my marriage.

Father, I pray for the courage to step fully into the identity You have given me. Like a sheep who knows the shepherds voice, attune my ear to Your word. When I falter, remind me that I am not defined by my mistakes but by Your mercy and grace. Lead me back to the path of my true identity. Thank You for walking alongside me, for never leaving or forsaking me, and for continually calling me back to who I was always meant to be.

In Jesus' name,

Amen.

2

THE IMPACT OF IDENTITY IN MARRIAGE

IN MY WORK as a marriage therapist, one of the most profound realizations I've seen again and again is this: identity affects everything, especially marriage. Who you believe you are shapes how you respond, how you communicate, how you love, and how you fight. When you live from a false identity, one built on fear, insecurity, shame, or the opinions of others, conflict becomes inevitable. But when you live from your true identity in Christ, everything shifts. Your posture changes. Your patterns change. And your marriage begins to flourish.

As Dr. Hardin notes in the foreword, conflict often pulls from deep-seated identity issues, those beliefs about who we are and how we're seen. This chapter explores what happens when we misunderstand identity, how it fuels conflict, and how God uses conflict as a part of His refining work, not to destroy us, but to draw us closer to who we really are in Him.

CONFLICT AS A MIRROR

Conflict in marriage is inevitable. But that doesn't make it a curse. In fact, conflict can be a gift, a mirror God uses to show us what's going on beneath the surface. We tend to see conflict as a problem to fix or avoid. God sees it as a tool for refining us, revealing where we've drifted from our true identity and inviting us back into alignment.

Conflict presses on the fractures we'd rather ignore. It stirs up the insecurities we've tried to bury. And it pulls to the surface the lies we've believed about ourselves for years, lies like:

- I'm not enough.
- I always mess things up.
- I have to defend myself or no one else will.
- If I'm not appreciated, I must not matter.

God doesn't just want to resolve your arguments. He wants to heal the wounds that keep creating them. And often, those wounds are tied directly to your false identity.

TWO INSECURITIES COLLIDING

Most conflict isn't really about what it appears to be. It might start with the trash, the tone, the unmet expectation, but underneath? It's often two insecurities colliding. When both spouses are operating out of fear or self-protection, they don't just misunderstand each other, they start to misinterpret each other's identity:

- A request becomes criticism.

- Silence becomes rejection.
- Needing space becomes abandonment.
- Feedback becomes failure.

I've seen this dynamic play out in my own marriage. A simple comment from Kristen, like pointing out something I forgot, would land in me like a deeper criticism. Not because she said it harshly, but because, deep down, I was already listening to the false narrative in my own head and it took me a while to realize it. I remember moments when I'd go out to grab lunch during work and think, *Kristen probably won't want anything from here,* so I wouldn't bring her anything back. Then I'd come home and hear, "It would've been nice to be thought of..." Her words weren't meant to be mean or attacking, but in that moment, they didn't feel small. Could she had worded her request for reassurance better, sure, but the issue within myself is that her words felt like confirmation of the lie I was already carrying: *You're not doing enough. You're letting her down. You're a failure as a husband.*

I immediately got defensive. I wanted to explain myself, to justify, to protect my ego. But the truth was, her words didn't create the wound, they just bumped into it. The wound translated her words in my head as "You clearly don't ever consider me." That's the power of false identity: it distorts the way we hear the people we love. It twists intention and fuels disconnection. And unless we name it, it keeps us stuck in the same defensive loop.

THE ROLE OF IDENTITY IN CONFLICT

When you're not rooted in your true identity, even the smallest disagreements can feel like a personal attack. Without the grounding of knowing who you are, every criticism cuts deeper. Every oversight feels intentional. Every disagreement threatens your worth. Piece by piece, insecurities replace trust until you hardly recognize the marriage you set sail with. The parts have changed, but what is it becoming, something anchored in truth, or adrift in fear?

False identity amplifies these moments by whispering lies like:

- "You're not enough."
- "You're unlovable."
- "You weren't worth protecting."
- "You're a failure."

These lies fuel defensiveness. They build emotional walls. They turn small issues into major battles, not because of what was said, but because of what was stirred up. You stop reacting to the moment, and start reacting to the fear underneath it. Suddenly, a simple comment about how the dishwasher was loaded or a heavy sigh over a forgotten errand becomes something more. It's not just about tasks, it's about identity.

Conflict reveals what false identities try to keep hidden. It exposes the lies we've internalized about ourselves and the insecurities that shape how we relate to each other. Conflict pulls up the narratives that have been planted in our minds, like the lie I believed that my value was based on how well I provided, and hearing Kristen feeling not considered immediately put me on the defensive.

But here's the good news: God didn't design conflict to break you down. He allows it to build you up. In His hands, conflict becomes a catalyst for healing. He doesn't mask symptoms, He reveals root causes. He doesn't just want peace on the surface, He wants restoration at the soul level.

THE GREAT PHYSICIAN

This reminds me of how God is often referred to as the Great Physician. A good doctor doesn't just treat the pain or mask the symptoms with a quick fix. They ask questions. They examine the source. They go deeper. God does the same with our marriages.

He's not interested in superficial harmony if it means we're still carrying wounds we've never addressed. God doesn't want temporary peace built on silence or distance. He wants real healing, at the root. God doesn't just diagnose the problem. Through conflict, He invites us into the solution. He wants to dig up the lies we've built our identity on and replace them with truth.

The lie says, *"You're not lovable."*

God says, *"You are My beloved."*

The lie says, *"You always fail."*

God says, *"I've given you everything you need for life and godliness."*

The lie says, *"You'll always be abandoned."*

God says, *"I will never leave you nor forsake you."*

God is revealing the false identity and inviting you into freedom. Meanwhile, of course, there's an enemy who sees the same moment and wants a very different outcome.

Where God sees opportunity, Satan sees an opening. Satan's strategy is always the same: twist conflict into isolation, turn wounds into resentment and make division feel safer than vulnerability.

God uses conflict to refine you. Satan tries to use it to accuse and divide you. That's why understanding what conflict really is, and what it reveals about identity, is so crucial. You're not just having a bad week. You're not just miscommunicating. You're being invited into a deeper process. A spiritual one.

> "The heart of man plans his way, but the
> Lord establishes his steps." Proverbs 16:9

Conflict is one of the ways God interrupts our plans. It's a divine wake-up call. A reminder that you are not your own. That you need Him. That you've been trying to operate in your own strength or prove your worth in the wrong ways. But through that disruption, God calls you back to who you really are. And from there, everything begins to heal.

REAL EXAMPLES

A wife, afraid of being abandoned because of childhood wounds or past hurts, begins to micromanage every detail. Maybe her parents divorced suddenly when she was a child, and no one explained why. Or perhaps she grew up in a home where love was inconsistent—affection one day, cold distance the next. She learned early that security was fragile, so she became hyper-vigilant. Her internal script says, *"If I don't control this, I'll lose him."* Or maybe, *"He will let this rela-*

tionship be ruined if I don't do something about it." What she sees as "protecting" the marriage is actually an attempt to manage her fear.

Her husband, feeling criticized and suffocated by her intensity, begins to emotionally withdraw. Maybe he grew up in a home where nothing he did was good enough. Where an A-minus was met with, "Why not an A?" or where his efforts to help were met with more correction than appreciation. Over time, he decided it was safer to keep his heart guarded than to keep trying and feel like a disappointment. So now, when his wife's control feels like mistrust, his internal script says, *"No matter what I do, I'll never be enough for her to trust me."*

Or as another example, a husband, fearful of failure because of wounds he's carried since adolescence, becomes overly focused on work or achievement. Maybe he grew up in a home where love felt conditional—where approval came only when he excelled in sports, grades, or responsibilities. Over time, he came to believe, *"If I'm not succeeding, I'm not good enough."* Now, as a husband, he throws himself into long hours at the office, home projects, or even ministry, not because he doesn't care about his wife, but because busyness and accomplishment keep the fear at bay.

His wife, meanwhile, begins to feel overlooked and unimportant. She might have grown up in a family where her needs were often brushed aside, or where she had to earn attention by being the "easy" or "low-maintenance" child. So now, when her husband seems unavailable or distracted, her internal script says, *"I don't matter enough to be chosen."* That ache for connection makes her start voicing her needs more urgently.

Again, he interprets her longing as criticism. She interprets his distraction as rejection. His pursuit of success feeds her loneliness. Her requests for connection feed his sense that he can't measure up. And again, they find themselves in a cycle—not reacting to each other's true hearts, but to the unhealed wounds they both carried into the marriage.

Now they're not reacting to each other, they are reacting to fear. Those fear-based narratives are the false identities playing out in their marriage. Instead of naming what's underneath, they stay locked in patterns. Her control feeds his withdrawal. His withdrawal reinforces her fear. And they both feel alone, unheard, and misunderstood.

The original conflict, maybe a budget disagreement or a parenting decision, is lost under the weight of false identity. They're not fighting over facts. They're fighting from wounds. And without awareness, they will keep creating more hurt in the very place they both want safety the most.

CONFLICT AS OPPORTUNITY

This is the power of false identity: it distorts your perception and amplifies your insecurities. But here's the hope, once you recognize the pattern, conflict becomes more than just a fight. It becomes a window. An opportunity.

It's no longer about who's right or who started it. Conflict isn't the enemy; it's the flashlight. It illuminates the part of your heart God wants to heal. It reveals the lies you've carried, the fears you've buried, and the story you've been telling yourself in silence. We spend so much of marriage reacting to how we feel: unseen, unworthy, unloved, instead of anchoring ourselves in what is true. As Martin Lloyd-Jones warned,

"The great lie of the devil is to make us think that the most important thing about us is how we feel about ourselves, rather than what we know to be true about God and His Word"

(LLOYD-JONES, 1965)

So the next time tension rises, don't just react. Pause and ask:

1. What lie am I believing about myself?
2. What insecurity is being triggered in me right now?
3. How is this impacting the way I'm treating my spouse?
4. What truth do I need to hold onto instead?

The goal is not to avoid conflict. It's to allow God to use it. When you trace conflict to its root, you stop fighting each other and start fighting for understanding. You shift from accusation to awareness. And suddenly, what felt like the thing tearing you apart becomes the very thing that draws you closer, if you let it.

A NEW WAY TO FIGHT

What if your next argument wasn't about who was right or wrong, but about uncovering a wound? What if, instead of letting false identities drive the narrative, you stepped back, named the lie, and reaffirmed who you are in Christ?

Let's be honest, that's not easy. In the heat of the moment, it's far more natural to defend yourself, point fingers, or shut down. But every conflict presents a choice:

- Let it drive a deeper wedge between you,
- Or use it to tear down the walls of insecurity and false identity.

That choice begins with humility. It's choosing to step back and ask God, "What's underneath this?" It's being honest about the deeper roots behind the surface tension. It's asking, not just reacting.

When you identify the false beliefs fueling the moment, conflict loses its power to divide. You disarm it. You create space for honesty. For empathy. For grace. And when your identity is rooted in Christ, not fear or insecurity, you become the stabilizing force in the relationship. That doesn't mean you're perfect. It means you are anchored. Because when your identity is secure, your presence becomes safe.

WHERE IT ALL STARTED

The insecurity and mistrust we feel in marriage today are echoes of Eden, where sin first fractured our connection with God and with each other. In the garden, Adam and Eve experienced perfect unity. No fear. No shame. No questioning their worth. They were naked and unashamed, not just physically but emotionally and spiritually. They lived from a secure identity: made in the image of God, fully known, fully loved.

The harmony they once knew gave way to blame,

shame, and mistrust, and those same dynamics ripple through every marriage today. They no longer saw each other through the lens of truth. They saw through a lens of fear. **Every argument we have, every misunderstanding, every defensive reaction or withdrawal, it all traces back to that moment in Eden when identity was fractured by sin.** When Adam and Eve stepped away from their true identity as God's image-bearers, insecurity, mistrust, and division entered the human story. Their fall didn't just break their relationship with God; it distorted how they saw themselves and each other.

ANCIENT WOUNDS, PRESENT HOPE

The fear of being enough. The need to control. The longing to be chosen. The ache to feel safe. These wounds aren't new. They're ancient, planted in Eden and passed down ever since. And unless you recognize them, you'll keep blaming your spouse for pain that started long before they came into your life.

This is why most couples try to fix behavior but miss the root. They say things like:

"We just need better communication."
"We're not on the same page."
"We're too different."

But more often than not, the real issue is that one or both spouses are living from a false identity. They're operating from insecurity, not intimacy. From fear, not faith. You can't heal what you won't name. And you can't change what you're still blaming on the surface. My relationship with my wife will never be improved through blame. It will only ever be improved through humility and ownership. Owning my wounds, my reactions, and the false identities I've let lead me. Until I take responsibility for what's broken in me, I'll keep trying to fix her instead of healing us.

This is where Genesis becomes more than history. It becomes a mirror. Yes, the Fall fractured us, but the story doesn't end there. Even in their sin, God sought them. Even in their shame, He called out, "Where are you?"

That same God is still calling. Still pursuing. Still offering covering for your shame and healing for your wounds. The gospel isn't just good news for your eternity. It's good news for your marriage. You don't fix your marriage by fixing your spouse. You heal your marriage by returning to who God says you are.

PREPARING FOR WHAT'S NEXT

Even now, after years of doing this work, those old insecurities still show up. I've had moments where I'm mid-argument and realize I'm not even reacting to the conversation. We're talking, but I'm defending something deeper, something old. That's the power of false identity. And that's why I've had to learn how to recognize it when it shows up.

In the next chapter, we'll go back to where it all started. We'll unpack what really happened in Eden and how it set the stage for the insecurities we wrestle with in our marriages today. To prepare for that, let's do a quick inventory.

Here are 10 common False Identities I see in marriages:

1. **"I'm not good enough."** – No matter what I do, it will never be enough.
2. **"I'm a failure."** – My mistakes define me; I'll never measure up.
3. **"I'm inadequate."** – I don't have what it takes to lead, provide, or succeed.
4. **"I'm unlovable."** – If people really knew me, they wouldn't accept me.
5. **"I'm only as valuable as what I achieve."** – My worth is tied to my performance.
6. **"I'm alone in this."** – No one understands or truly has my back.
7. **"I'm not as important as other people."** – What I bring to the table doesn't really matter.
8. **"I'm too broken to be used by God."** – My past disqualifies me from purpose.
9. **"I'm weak if I show emotion."** – If I open up, I'll be seen as less of a man.
10. **"I'm not worthy of respect."** – I have to constantly prove myself to be taken seriously.

As we step into the next chapter, hold these close. You can't challenge what you haven't named. And healing begins where truth enters in.

Go Deeper With These Verses

Ephesians 4:15–16, Colossians 3:12, Galatians 2:20,
Romans 12:2

APPLICATION

As a therapist, I often guide clients through the process of rediscovering their true identity. These steps aren't just theoretical. I've watched them change marriages. I've seen men soften when they stop trying to prove their worth and start receiving God's truth. I've seen couples reconnect, not because the problem disappeared, but because they finally started hearing each other through a different lens.

Take a few minutes to reflect on the identity you most often live from in marriage:

• When conflict arises, who do you become?

• What do you fear your spouse sees in you?

• What do you believe about yourself that might not be true?

Now contrast that with what God says about you in Scripture. Choose one verse from the list above or another identity verse in the Bible and write it somewhere you'll see it regularly. Use it as a reminder that your actions don't determine your identity, but your identity in Christ should reshape your actions.

Write out a short script: "Next time I feel __, I want to remember that I am __ in Christ, and I will choose to __ instead."

———

Pray This:

Father,

Help me stop living from a false identity.

I confess that too often I let fear, failure, or insecurity define me in my marriage. I try to protect myself, prove myself, or withdraw completely.

Remind me that I am Yours, chosen, called, and loved. Teach me to live from that place of security. Let my words, reactions, and presence in my marriage be shaped by who I am in You, not by who I'm afraid I might be.

Make me an anchor of grace in my home. Give me the courage to lay down the old ways of reacting and to step into the new life You've already given me.

In Jesus' name,

Amen.

3

THE GENESIS OF CONFLICT

INSECURITY HAS A BEGINNING. Its roots trace back to the Garden of Eden, where the enemy's first deception introduced fear, shame, and mistrust into the human heart. Genesis 3 isn't just a story about the fall, it's a moment that explains why we struggle the way we do. It reveals the origin of the false identities we carry and shows us that the need for healing didn't begin with us. It began the moment we lost sight of who we were created to be.

THE LIE THAT BIRTHED INSECURITY

In the beginning, Adam and Eve walked in perfect unity with God, with creation, and with each other. They didn't question their worth or wonder if they measured up. Their identities were secure, rooted in the voice of their Creator. There was no striving, no fear of being misunderstood, no shame about being fully seen. They walked in the garden with nothing to hide, living in the fullness of who they were.

Then another voice entered the garden. A voice that didn't belong to God. A voice that approached Eve with malicious intent. The serpent's words were deliberate and laced with deception: "Did God *really* say, 'You shall not eat of any tree in the garden'?" (Genesis 3:1, ESV). It wasn't an outright denial of God's Word but a subtle seed of doubt. A seed that planted doubt in Eve's mind causing her to question God's goodness, His intentions, and her place in His creation. Eve responded, but the serpent kept twisting. "You will not surely die...you will be like God, knowing good and evil" (Genesis 3:4-5, ESV).

In that moment, the lie took root: **"You are not enough as you are. You are missing something essential. And if you want to be whole, you'll have to take it for yourself."** Eve believed that lie. The lie that created a fracture in her trust, not only in God but also in her identity as one perfectly made in His image. She saw the fruit differently now. No longer as something forbidden, but as desirable, as the key to something she was supposedly missing, and she took it.

Adam, meanwhile, was there. Silent. Watching. He didn't lead, protect, or speak. He didn't remind Eve of what God had said. He didn't call the serpent out or push back against the lie. He stood by, passive, absent in the moment when his presence was most needed. His silence left Eve vulnerable. His inaction allowed deception to go unchallenged. His failure to engage opened the door for brokenness, not only for their marriage, but for every marriage that would come after.

HIDING IN THE SHADOW OF SHAME

The immediate result of eating the fruit wasn't the empowerment the serpent had promised; it was fear and shame. Sin entered the world and with it, everything fractured. The divide formed by sin was filled with insecurity, the natural condition of creation separated from the Creator. Adam and Eve's relationship with God was severed, and their connection with each other was marred by blame and mistrust. Suddenly, they realized their nakedness. What once symbolized openness and unity now represented vulnerability and inadequacy.

Insecurity entered the human heart the moment sin distorted the truth about who we are and who God is. While this account doesn't explicitly name 'insecurity,' we see its fruit immediately after the Fall: hiding, shame, blame, and fear. These responses suggest a rupture in identity, what we now call insecurity. We are entering Adam and Eve's emotional experience with humility, not certainty, but the pattern is unmistakable.

Eve's wound was rooted in the fear of being unprotected and unloved. Her insecurity told her, *"You need to take control to protect yourself because no one else will."* Adam's wound was rooted in the shame of failing to lead and the fear of losing respect. His insecurity told him, *"You've failed, and now you are unworthy of respect and trust."* These insecurities didn't stay in the garden. They became foundational struggles in relationships to this day.

Their physical nakedness mirrored a deeper spiritual vulnerability. They were no longer secure in their relationship with God or with each other. When God called to them, they hid, covering their nakedness with fig leaves. An act of desperation born from fear and guilt. Adam's response to God's call, "I heard you in the garden, and I was afraid because I was naked, so I hid" (Genesis 3:10), reflects what many of us feel when faced with our own insecurities: fear and shame that lead to avoidance and isolation.

When confronted by God, their responses revealed the deep cracks in their unity. Adam deflected responsibility, blaming Eve and even God Himself: "The woman *you* gave to be with me—she gave me some fruit from the tree, and I ate" (Genesis 3:12). Eve pointed to the serpent: "The serpent deceived me, and I ate" (Genesis 3:13). Instead of owning their sin, they turned against one another, sowing seeds of division that would ripple through every relationship to come. The harmony they once enjoyed was replaced with blame, fear, and defensiveness.

Hiding is the natural response to insecurity, but God doesn't leave us in the bushes. Just as He called Adam and Eve out of hiding, He calls us out of the shadows of our shame. God knows that our tendency is to hide, to cover ourselves with flimsy solutions to mask the deeper wounds. But He lovingly confronts us, bringing our vulnerabilities into the light, not to shame us further, but to heal and redeem.

THE CONSEQUENCE

Before we can understand the gravity of consequences given by God in response to Adam and Eve's sin, we need to understand the divine strategy revealed later in Scripture, specifically through Paul's words in Ephesians 5. Often misunderstood or misapplied, this chapter offers a power-ful, healing picture of God's design for marriage.

Paul directly addresses husbands to "love your wives, as Christ loved the church and gave himself up for her" (Eph-esians 5:25, ESV). It's a command that resonates with clarity and purpose, and it's one I wholeheartedly support. What's striking is that when Paul addresses the wives, he doesn't offer the same command to love in return. Instead, he calls wives to respect and submit to their husbands.

Why is this? Does this imply that wives don't need to love their husbands? Certainly not. This doesn't mean love is unimportant for wives. It actually reveals something deeper. Something that connects back to Eden. Paul's distinction is not arbitrary. It speaks to the unique wounds and insecurities introduced by sin, and the divine path toward those wounds.

In Paul's time, men were viewed as the primary leaders, protectors, and providers. Women often held limited roles and rights, largely dependent on male figures for social standing and safety. In that context, telling husbands to love their wives as Christ loved the church wasn't just counter-cultural, it was revolutionary. It called men to a level of sacrificial love and spiritual leadership that was anything but passive. It highlighted the need for genuine affection and godliness in marriage. It called them to reverse Adam's failure in the garden.

Let's go back to Genesis 3 and trace the connection. Eve is approached by the serpent, the deceiver, who tempts her to eat from the tree of knowledge of good and evil. As we read closely, we see that Adam was right there next to Eve throughout this whole event. Adam was complicit and complacent in that moment. This is the origin of Eve's insecurity, her wound. She was threatened, deceived, lied to, and manipulated. And her protector, lover, and teammate stood silent, allowing it to happen and allowing Eve to bring sin into the world.

Furthermore, when God calls attention to the presence of sin, Adam's response was defensiveness. This response was a betrayal and abandonment that cut a deep wound into the heart of Eve, a wound that transcends all womankind for generations. Eve wasn't just deceived, she was abandoned. And when the consequence came, he turned on her in an ultimate sign of betrayal. This response lacked the love that husbands are instructed to have, a love that models Christ's love for the church.

This is the origin of a wound that many women carry to this day. The fear of being unprotected, unloved, and blamed. Eve's response was shaped by betrayal and abandonment. Moving forward in Genesis 3, God reveals how sin would affect relationships between husbands and wives. To Eve, God said, "Your desire will be for your husband, and he will rule over you" (Genesis 3:16). That one verse captures the relational tension born from sin. A wife, grasping for security, and a husband, tempted to dominate rather than lovingly lead. Both are acting from insecurity. Both are trying to fill a void that only God can fill.

Adam, too, bore a consequence. He would now struggle with feelings of inadequacy and a desire to overcompensate feelings of failure while trying to reclaim the respect he had lost. These insecurities set the stage for conflict, not just between Adam and Eve, but for all marriages to come. Sound familiar?

This passage in Genesis reveals more than punishment. It exposes the relational fracture between men and women. It shows us how sin created new instincts: passivity in the husband, control in the wife. Fear took the place of unity. Pride took the place of partnership.

But here's the key: God didn't implant insecurity into Adam and Eve. He simply revealed what now existed in them because of sin. The consequence wasn't only sweat and pain, it was a severed sense of identity. A broken awareness of who they were and how they were meant to relate to one another.

When we return to Ephesians 5 with this understanding, Paul's words come into focus with greater depth. He's not just giving marital advice. He's offering a divine remedy. Husbands are called to love with initiative, self-sacrifice, and spiritual leadership. The very things Adam failed to do. Wives are called to respect and trust, countering the fear and control born from betrayal. This is not about rigid gender roles or transactional submission. It's about healing. It's about redemption. Paul's instruction is meant to be restorative. **It is heaven's answer to Eden's fracture.**

The solution to this deep-seated issue is found in Jesus Christ's perfect sacrifice. His act of love on the cross reaches the very roots of our fallen nature, offering healing and restoration. Through Him, the relationship between husbands and wives is reconciled, reflecting God's original design for marriage based on love, respect, and mutual submission.

GOD'S IMMEDIATE PLAN OF REDEMPTION

The beauty of Genesis 3 isn't just in its honesty about human failure, it is found in God's immediate response. He doesn't abandon Adam and Eve in their shame. He doesn't leave them to fix what they've broken. Instead, he initiates a plan of redemption that foreshadows the ultimate sacrifice of Jesus.

When Adam and Eve tried to cover their shame with fig leaves, God replaced their inadequate coverings with garments made from animal skins (Genesis 3:21). That moment gets me every time. Even in judgment, God moves toward them with mercy. He doesn't abandon them to their fig leaves. He covers them. This act required the shedding of blood, an unmistakable foreshadowing of Christ's sacrifice. **God's plan of redemption and salvation is bigger than our fears and insecurities.** From the very beginning, God made it clear: our shame wouldn't be covered by our efforts, but by His.

This act of covering was more than provision. It was prophecy. It was a picture of the gospel. Just as God clothed Adam and Eve, Jesus would one day clothe us in righteousness. What Adam and Eve could not do for themselves, God did for them. What we cannot do for ourselves, Jesus has done for us. When our insecurities cause us to question our identity, God reminds us that we are His creation.

LOVE AND RESPECT—THE BIBLICAL BLUEPRINT

The insecurity and mistrust we feel today are echoes of Eden. That moment in the garden set the stage for every fear of rejection, every need to prove ourselves, and every instinct to hide. But just as God initiated redemption then, He continues that work today, healing and restoring us through Christ.

Ephesians 5 offers a profound answer to the relational wounds introduced by sin. Paul's call for husbands to love and wives to respect is not about enforcing rigid roles or hierarchy. It's about healing the fracture. Love and respect are not simply nice ideas or cultural suggestions; they are divinely inspired principles designed to counteract the wounds of sin and foster unity in marriage.

In the next chapter, we'll take a closer look at this biblical blueprint. What does it really mean for a husband to love his wife as Christ loves the church? And how does a wife's respect create the foundation for mutual trust and intimacy? Together, we'll explore how these principles, when embraced, can transform your marriage. I've seen this blueprint transform marriages, including my own. Not because we get it perfect, but because we're learning to return to the One who does. And the more we return, the more we begin to recognize each other not as enemies, but as image-bearers.

———

Go Deeper With These Verses:

Genesis 3:6–13, Romans 5:12, 1 John 4:18, Hebrews 4:13

APPLICATION:

Read Genesis 3 and identify which patterns show up most in
your marriage:

- Hiding
- Blame
- Control
- Passivity
- Shame

Then ask yourself:

- When do I default to this pattern?
- What does it cost me and my spouse?
- What would it look like to replace it with
  presence, responsibility, or vulnerability?

Journal a one-paragraph prayer confessing your most
common fallback, and ask for the courage to step out of it.

Pray This:

Father,

I see in Adam and Eve what I see in myself, fear, blame, and a desire to hide.

I want to be known, but I also fear what will happen when I'm fully seen.

Help me stop covering up with control, silence, or criticism. Show me how to step into vulnerability, even when it's uncomfortable. Let Your love replace the fear that drives distance in my marriage.

Thank You for covering my shame with grace and inviting me back into relationship with You, and with my spouse.

In Jesus' name, Amen.

4

LOVE AND RESPECT: A BIBLICAL BLUEPRINT

ONE OF THE frustrations I often hear from couples is this: *"If I have to ask for love, care, or support, it doesn't feel as meaningful."* Maybe you've felt that too. When love has to be requested, it can feel like it wasn't freely given. The doubt creeps in. Do they really care? Or are they just responding out of pressure?

For many women, love is felt most deeply when it is expressed through pursuit. They want to be noticed without having to wave a flag. They want to be cherished, prioritized, and chosen without prompting. Pursuit or proactive love tells them they matter. That they're not just a task or a role. That they are loved without conditions. This touches the wound left by Adam's silence in the garden. When love only shows up as a response or is just reactive, it can feel more like obligation than desire.

For many men, respect is experienced through responsiveness. When their efforts are acknowledged, when their ideas are heard, when their presence is affirmed, it communicates worth. They don't need applause. But when they're met with contempt or dismissal, it chips away at their sense of identity. Respect often shows up in the little things: a nod of agreement, a word of trust, a willingness to listen. Or in many cases, respect speaks the loudest in what is withheld, criticism, sarcasm, or correction.

This core difference, proactive pursuit versus responsive affirmation, creates tension in so many marriages. A husband may not understand why his wife feels neglected when he waits for her to ask. A wife may not realize how much her tone affects his confidence and connection. Most of the time, the love is there. But it's being expressed in a language the other person doesn't understand. Or in some cases the message of love is muted underneath layers of hurt.

I've lived this. There have been seasons in my marriage where I didn't understand why Kristen felt unseen. In my mind, I was showing up. I was working, providing, being present. But I wasn't pursuing. I wasn't reminding her that she mattered outside of our shared responsibilities. And when she called attention to this reality, I felt disrespected. This would cause me to withdraw, not because I didn't love her, but because I didn't feel safe offering love when I didn't feel seen either. The more I stayed tied to the false identity that my worth depended on her emotions, the more stuck I became.

The cycle is real. But it can be broken. And that's where Scripture gives us something more than just generic relationship advice. It gives up a blueprint. This isn't about stereotypes or formulas or who is right or wrong. It's about paying attention to how your spouse is wired and stepping into your role in a way that builds intimacy and trust.

THE BIBLICAL CALL TO LOVE AND RESPECT

Ephesians 5 is often quoted in marriage circles, but it's rarely understood in full. Paul writes,*"Husbands, love your wives, as Christ loved the church and gave himself up for her"* (Ephesians 5:25, ESV). Yet, when Paul addresses wives, he doesn't reciprocate with a command to *love* their husbands. Instead, he tells them to *respect* their husbands (Ephesians 5:33).

This isn't about who has more value. It's not about hierarchy. It's a healing strategy. Paul, led by the Holy Spirit, is speaking into the wounds introduced in Eden. The wounds that still echo in modern marriages.

SUBMISSION: NOT CONTROL, BUT COVENANT

Much of the tension surrounding submission stems from a misunderstanding of what it truly means. Many interpret submission as blind obedience, a loss of identity, or a relinquishing of personal agency. But submission doesn't mean losing your voice. It doesn't mean agreeing with everything. Biblical submission is a willing posture of respect. It says, "I trust you enough to partner with you, to listen, to support." It is strength choosing partnership over control.

But let's be clear, submission is not automatic. My wife is far more likely to trust my leadership when she sees that I am consistently submitting myself to Jesus. When I am led by Christ I become someone who is safe to follow. My decisions are not rooted in pride or self-interest, but in prayer, humility, and sacrificial love. The more I lay myself down before the Lord, the more my wife can trust that she won't have to fight for her place in the marriage.

Jesus modeled submission perfectly. He wasn't coerced. He yielded to the Father out of love and unity. He remained fully powerful, fully worthy, and yet fully surrendered. When wives are called to submit, it is not about weakness. It's an invitation to mirror the same trust in a husband who is called to lead like Christ, with sacrificial love, not domination.

And leading, in this context, is not about authority. It's about responsibility. A husband is called to lead in love. To go first in humility. To consider his wife's needs before his own. To lay down ego for the sake of unity.

THE CYCLE OF MISUNDERSTANDING

When my wife feels unloved, respect becomes harder for her to give. When I feel disrespected, love becomes hard to for me to offer. And the cycle begins. Hurt creates silence. Silence creates distance. Distance creates resentment. It's a loop that doesn't resolve itself unless someone chooses to go first.

I remember one particular night where we were both off the path of our true identity. Nothing huge had happened. Just tension. I had been short with her earlier, distracted and irritable. She pulled back emotionally. I sensed the distance but didn't know how to fix it. I was waiting for her to show warmth again so I could relax. She was waiting for me to show love again so she could feel safe. She broke the silent tension by criticizing my lack of affection in her moments of need. "Why is it so hard to hug someone you love?" Meanwhile, I processed the moment very differently. "How am I supposed to comfort her if I can't even get close without getting burned?" That moment stuck with me because it revealed how easy it is to get stuck waiting for the other to move first.

CONFLICT ISN'T THE PROBLEM, AVOIDANCE IS

Conflict is not a sign of a broken marriage. It's a sign that two people are still trying to matter to each other. The danger isn't in fighting. It's in avoiding. When couples stop fighting altogether, it often means they've stopped hoping for something better.

James tells us to "Count it all joy when we face trails," because trials produces steadfastness. That applies to marriage too. Conflict handled in the flesh, leads to pride, blame, and distance. But conflict handled in faith leads to connection, healing and depth. The difference isn't whether you fight, it's how you fight.

Proverbs says "A soft answer turns away wrath." Jesus modeled this perfectly. He never avoided hard conversations, but He always held truth and grace together. Marriage needs that same balance. Truth and grace.

Avoiding conflict doesn't protect the relationship. It pushes the wound underground. It allows small fractures to deepen in silence. But when conflict is met with humility, responsibility and openness, it becomes a turning point. Not the end of intimacy but the beginning of it.

FORGIVENESS: THE FIGHT FOR FREEDOM

Every couple will face a moment where forgiveness is necessary. Not always because of something catastrophic, but because we are human. We fail. We hurt each other. And when that happens, the question becomes: Will you let the wound lead, or will you let grace go first?

The natural instinct is to wait for the other person to apologize first. They should admit they were wrong. They should change before I forgive. But forgiveness doesn't work like that. If it did, we would all be doomed. God didn't wait for us to deserve forgiveness. "While we were still sinners, Christ died for us" (Romans 5:8). Translate that verse to your own marriage. "While my wife is still messing up, I will forgive her." Or "While my husband still hasn't figured out what he is doing wrong, I will forgive him." If God based forgiveness on our worthiness, we would still be lost. But He forgave first. And in marriage, we are called to do the same.

Forgiveness isn't saying what happened was okay. It's not pretending the hurt didn't matter. It's not removing accountability. Forgiveness is releasing the debt. It's placing justice in God's hands. It's saying, "I refuse to let this wound control me anymore." It's trusting that God is bigger than your pain.

THE DIFFERENCE BETWEEN FRUIT AND POISON

Imagine two couples. The first chooses to forgive. Not because it's easy, but because they trust God more than their emotions. They don't excuse each other's faults, but they don't keep score either. They extend grace, even when it's undeserved. They remember marriage is bigger than any single offense. Their home is subsequently filled with peace, intimacy and safety.

The second couple holds onto their grievances like weapons. Every mistake is relived. Every wound reopened.

Their home becomes a battleground. They might still live under the same roof, but emotionally, they are miles apart.

What's the difference? Forgiveness brings healing. Bitterness brings decay. A marriage poisoned by resentment cannot survive. A marriage built on grace can withstand anything.

A HISTORICAL LESSON IN ESCALATING OFFENSE

History offers a vivid reminder of how pride and unhealed wounds can turn a small offense into an all-out war. In the early 18th century, tensions between Britain and Spain simmered in the Caribbean. British merchants frequently clashed with Spanish coast guards who were determined to control trade in the region. In 1731, a Spanish patrol boarded a British merchant ship commanded by Captain Robert Jenkins. In a heated search, they accused Jenkins of smuggling and, as punishment, severed his ear.

For years, Jenkins' injury remained a personal wound, an injustice, but not yet a cause for war. That changed when he appeared before the British Parliament in 1738, holding his preserved ear in a jar as evidence of Spanish cruelty. This single, visible wound became a symbol, fuel for national pride and a rallying cry for vengeance. Parliament, gripped by this vivid image of humiliation, declared war on Spain in 1739. A severed ear had become the catalyst for a conflict that would drag on for nearly a decade, costing countless lives.

The lesson is clear: when an offense is left to fester, pride and insecurity can turn it into something far more destructive. Jenkins' ear was real, but the real war wasn't about the ear. It was about the refusal to let go of an offense, the pride and pain that turned a moment into a movement.

RETURNING TO THE HEART OF MARRIAGE

In marriage, it's rarely a single harsh word or moment of neglect that causes the deepest wounds. It's the story we attach to that moment and the refusal to let it go. Pride says, "I shouldn't have to be the one to forgive." Fear says, "If I let this go, they'll never learn." Insecurity says, "Their failure means I'm not enough." But God says, "Forgive as I have forgiven you."

Forgiveness doesn't minimize the pain. It simply refuses to let that pain have the final word. The War of Jenkins' Ear reminds us that the real battle is never just outside of us. It's within, between pride and humility, self-protection and selfless love. And the only way to break the cycle is to choose the kind of love that doesn't keep score, the kind of grace that isn't based on worthiness, and the kind of forgiveness that reflects the heart of God.

Too many of us are walking around with an ear in a jar. We hold onto our wounds with bitterness to the point where our home becomes a battleground and the casualties of war are not only our marriages but the security of our children. We become responsible for our children's false identities and insecurities created in that battleground.

HOW UNFORGIVENESS DISTORTS FAITH

The longer bitterness lingers, the more likely it is to be spiritualized. We use our faith to justify a hardened heart. It shows up in subtle ways:

1. Using faith as a moral high ground

- "I'll forgive when they act more like a godly spouse."
- "They need to prove they've changed."
- "If they really loved Jesus, they wouldn't have done that."

That's not forgiveness. That's control dressed up as righteousness. We're not called to forgive when they earn it. We're called to forgive because God forgave us first.

2. Holding their past against them in the name of accountability

- "I forgive you, but I'll never let you forget it."
- "You owe me now."
- "You need to keep proving yourself if you want to be trusted."

That's not biblical accountability. That's punishment. Love keeps no record of wrongs (1 Corinthians 13:5).

3. Justifying a hard heart in the name of truth

- "I won't let them off the hook."
- "They need to feel the weight of what they did."
- "They don't deserve to move on yet."

But Jesus never withheld grace. If you use "truth" to excuse your bitterness, you've missed the heart of the gospel. Sometimes, this misuse of faith isn't just about controlling the situation, it's also about protecting a false identity. When someone uses faith as a weapon, it doesn't come from spiritual strength. It comes from insecurity. They're living from fear and hurt, not from the security of who they are in Christ. They're wearing their faith as armor to shield themselves instead of allowing it to transform them from the inside out. And while God can absolutely protect you, true faith, rooted in the love of Christ, doesn't need to control, it heals and sets free.

FORGIVENESS IS BETWEEN YOU AND GOD

Your spouse may never apologize the way you want or say the right words. They may never fully understand the pain they caused. But forgiveness isn't about them. It's about your obedience to God. It's about trusting that God sees you, hears you, and will handle justice better than you ever could.

Forgiveness is your responsibility, not theirs. You are called to be a conduit of the forgiveness already given to you by God through the sacrifice of Jesus on the cross. Are you going to withhold the eternal gift that God has given you by refusing to extend it to others? When you forgive, you're not letting them off the hook. You're letting yourself off the hook. You're choosing freedom over control. You're choosing peace over resentment. You're choosing to be shaped by grace, not bitterness. You're saying, "God I trust You to carry what I can't."

So the real question isn't, "Do they deserve forgiveness?" The real question is, "Am I willing to trust God with this wound?"

Because that decision shapes the marriage you build. And it shapes the person you become.

WRAP UP

There was a time recently when I was on the receiving end of some pretty heavy emotionally charged text messages from a friend. The passion he spoke from was palpable and it twisted the intended message into an attack. He was feeling scared and needed reassurance but what was communicated was accusation, judgement, and name calling. While hearing words and phrases like "hypocrite", "how could you", "if that's what you believe than we can't be friends", a massive trigger of defensiveness was alerted within me. It was one of the few times in my life where I felt like my faith was truly being put to the test and was under attack. What I can only attribute as a leading of the Holy Spirit, I remained calm and validating. For every triggering message that came my way, I remembered that a relationship is more important that how someone else's emotional reaction makes me feel.

If I responded with defensiveness or a counter-attack, it would be hard for me to not accept the label as hypocrite. I claim to be a Christ follower and if I respond to attack with an attack, where am I putting my faith, because in that moment it would've been in my circumstances not Jesus. So I responded to my friend in the best way I could while remembering what it means to show grace. I told him, "I hear you, I can see how strongly you feel about this and I appreciate your willingness to share this with me... Your friendship matters to me and so does how you feel..." (paraphrased for clarity).

———

Go Deeper With These Verses

Ephesians 5:21–33, 1 Peter 3:7, 1 Corinthians 13:4–7, Philippians 2:3–5

———

APPLICATION:

Ask your spouse this question:

"*When do you feel most loved by me? When do you feel most respected?*"

Then, reflect on your answer to this:

- Do I give what I most want to receive?
- Am I loving from identity or insecurity?
- Where do I need to reorient my role in the relationship to reflect Christ?

Choose one specific way this week to *pursue* your spouse, no strings attached.

———

Pray This:

Lord,

It's easy to love when things are good, but harder when tension rises.

I confess that at times I lead with pride, not patience. I respond with selfishness instead of sacrifice.

Teach me what it looks like to love and respect from a place of wholeness. Let my marriage reflect not perfection, but pursuit, of You and of each other.

Give me the humility to serve, the courage to lead, and the strength to love unconditionally.

In Jesus' name, Amen.

5

THE HUSBAND'S CALL: SACRIFICIAL LOVE

YOU CAN'T LEAD your marriage well until you've learned how to lay yourself down. Not disappear. Not perform. Not manage. Lay yourself down.

There's a difference between laying yourself down and losing yourself. Sacrificial love flows from a place of identity. Performative love tries to earn it. One is rooted in strength, the other in fear. I've done both. There were seasons in my marriage when I was doing all the "right" things, but the motivation underneath was anxiety. I wasn't leading Kristen in love. I was managing her moods, trying to keep the peace, trying not to fail or make things worse. And while it might've looked like love on the surface, it was actually fear dressed up as leadership.

This chapter isn't about effort or how much you provide. It's about identity. It's not about getting credit for trying hard. It's about becoming the kind of man who leads like Christ, strong enough to love sacrificially, secure enough to serve. Because there will be moments in your life and marriage where you hit a fork in the road. You'll have to choose between sacrifice or self. You'll have to decide if you're going to lead with courage and trust God or protect your comfort.

And I can tell you with certainty: I have never regretted trusting God. But there are plenty of times in my life where I wish I would have trusted Him more, especially in my marriage. When I chose pride over presence, or when I stayed comfortable instead of showing up, I missed what mattered most. Most men don't avoid sacrifice because it's painful. We avoid it because we've built our identity around what might be taken from us, circumstances.

So if you're struggling to give something up like your job, your comfort, or your freedom, maybe it's time to ask the harder question: Do I value this more than the person I was called to love?

If giving up the job feels like failure, it's probably because you've tied your identity to it. But sacrifice rooted in Christ never leads to loss. It leads to growth. Even with that reassurance, it's not easy to do. If it were easy, it wouldn't be called a sacrifice.

FROM FALSE IDENTITY TO SACRIFICIAL LOVE

Sometimes we know exactly what love requires of us in our marriage. We know what needs to be said. We know the gentle response that should be given. We even know the sacrifice needed. But something inside of us resists. It's like a gravitational pull back toward selfishness, defensiveness, pride, or avoidance. We know what love looks like, but we don't always choose it.

This comes from false identity and it creates a gap between what we believe and how we behave. And it's the greatest roadblock to sacrificial love.

If you've ever wondered, *"Why do I keep reacting like this when I know better?"* You're not crazy. You're just human. False identity has a way of convincing us we're safer when we protect, defend, or retreat. But nothing about Christ's love was self-protective. He didn't flinch from the cost. He embraced it. This is exactly why the call to husbands is so important. Because when you try to love from an insecurity, you're always reacting. But when you love from your true identity, you're leading.

In the last chapter, I talked about how easy it was for me to tie my self-worth to Kristen's mood. If she was happy, I felt like I was doing great. If she was upset, I took it as proof that I'm not good enough and I'm failing. And if I can't handle that feeling of failure, I would defend myself. I would try to convince her why she shouldn't feel the way she does. I would get stuck in the loop: either I prove myself, or I protect myself. That's not sacrificial love.

Every man wants to provide. And for many husbands, provision isn't just financial, it's personal. We feel responsible for her peace of mind, her happiness, her security. I found that one of the areas it was hardest for me to not spiral in my insecurity and stay consistent was when Kristen would share her dreams and aspirations with me. When she started talking about dreams, where she wants to go, what she hopes for, what she wishes we could afford, something flared up in me.

"If I can't give her those things, I've failed."
"If she's dreaming of something more, it means
    I'm not enough."
"If I don't figure this out, she won't stay."

That fear isn't just about money. It's about identity. It's the voice of insecurity saying: *"You're only valuable if you can deliver."* I didn't hear dreams, I heard pressure. I felt like I was being measured. Compared. I felt like I was failing. That's how insecurity speaks. It filters hope through fear and turns vision into shame.

And that mindset didn't start with a paycheck. It started in the Garden. When sin entered the world, Adam didn't just experience separation from God, he experienced insecurity in his role.

- He was created to cultivate. Now the ground fights back.
- He was called to lead. Now his leadership feels questioned.
- He was made to walk with God. Now he hides in fear and shame.

That fracture gave birth to what many men carry today: a capability-based insecurity.

> *"I am what I can achieve."*
> *"If I can't fix it, I'm worthless."*
> *"If I don't do it right, I don't deserve to lead."*

So we try harder. We grind. We hustle. We live in silent fear that we're not measuring up, so we overcompensate by doing more. But this only deepens the lie: *"I need to do in order to be."* **But That's Not the Gospel.** The gospel flips that script: *"I am, therefore I do."* You're not a man because you can provide. You're a man because you were created in

God's image, redeemed by Christ, and called to love like Him.

From that place of security, you do—

- not to prove,
- not to earn,
- but because it flows out of who you already are.

This doesn't make you passive. It makes you powerful. Because when your actions are rooted in identity, they're not reactive, they're intentional. They're no longer about *you*, they're about *love*.

REFRAMING HER DREAMS

Now back to her dreams. There were times when the bills were easily covered, and suddenly Kristen would start dreaming. "Wouldn't it be fun to take the kids there?" or "Maybe we could upgrade this?" Her eyes would light up, and possibilities felt endless. But then we've had seasons where we were just trying to keep the lights on, when every dollar was spoken for, and every conversation felt heavy. In those moments, the dreaming stopped. Not because she didn't want to hope, but because it felt dangerous to.

And that's when it hit me: her dreaming isn't a sign that I'm not doing enough. It's actually evidence that I've helped create enough stability for her to feel safe imagining again. Her dreams don't have to be threats. They can be signs of security.

Dreaming is risky. It requires emotional margin. So if your wife is dreaming, it might not be a sign that she's demanding more from you. It might be a sign that she trusts what you've built enough to let her imagination breathe again.

So don't rush to shut down the dream. And don't interpret it as a jab at your performance. Instead, ask: *"Is this dream a sign that she feels safe enough to want again?"*

If it is, that's not failure. That's fruit. It's evidence that God is already working beneath the surface. And this is where the real shift begins: once the false belief is exposed, you have a choice. You can keep reacting out of fear. Or you can lead from love, posturing yourself in submission to God and trusting in Him with your marriage. Sacrificial love says, "Even when she's upset, I will stay steady. Even when I feel misunderstood, I will stay open."

This kind of love doesn't come from willpower. It comes from knowing who you are in Christ. This is why I continually remind my clients that **a lack of confidence in who you are leads to a lack of consistency in what you do.** If your identity rises and falls with her reactions, then your love will always be inconsistent. But when your identity is secure, then your love can be stable, even when the environment isn't. That's what sacrificial love looks like. Staying when it's hard. Listening when you feel attacked. Speaking gently when you want to withdraw. Leading even when you feel empty.

THE BLUEPRINT: CHRIST'S LOVE IN ACTION

Jesus didn't just die for the church. He lived for her. He washed feet. He gave time. He protected. He corrected with tenderness. He prayed for her. He moved first, every time. He never made her beg for affection. He didn't wait until it was convenient. He didn't love based on performance. He loved because it was His nature to love. That's the blueprint.

Some men think they're leading because they're in charge. But biblical leadership isn't about control, it's about care. You're not the head of your marriage so you can get your way. You're the head so you can lay yourself down.

That means:

- Going first in forgiveness.
- Going first in humility.
- Going first in hard conversations.
- Going first in sacrifice.

Ephesians 5 doesn't just say, "Love your wife." It says, "Love her as Christ loved the church." That means you don't get to lead by comfort. You lead by cross. And the more rooted you are in your identity in Christ, the less you'll need to prove yourself. Strong men don't have to dominate the room to feel powerful. They're powerful because they know who they are, and they lead from that truth.

So ask yourself: If your wife has to initiate emotional connection, what story is that telling her? If she's the one carrying the weight of keeping the relationship close, how long before she feels alone in a marriage that was meant to be a partnership?

Leadership does't mean you make the final call and the authority is yours, it means you make the first move. Are you showing up in a way that makes her feel safe enough to open up? Are you creating an environment where she can flourish or one where she feels like she has to shrink to keep the peace. Or maybe what will resonate more, does your wife have to amplify her reactions in conversations in order to get you to take her emotional needs more serious. You may be in a season of your marriage where you are exhausted from hearing your wife's criticism, complaints, or nagging. What you likely don't realize is those behaviors in her are symptomatic of a lack of leadership. Dr. Sue Johnson would say that people tend to amplify their emotional reactions as a way to compensate for their partner's lack of emotional responsibility (Johnson, 2013).

Imagine this: Someone's standing at the edge of a pool, afraid to jump in. What helps them most? Do you yell from the side, "Just jump already." Do you sit next to them and say, "it's not that bad"? No. You jump in first. You show them it's safe. You lead by example.

That's exactly what Jesus did with Peter.

Peter didn't walk on water because Jesus sat in the boat coaching him from the sidelines. He walked because Jesus was already out there, walking. It was an invitation wrapped in example. That's leadership. That's sacrificial love.

Your wife doesn't need pressure. She needs presence. She doesn't need instruction. She needs demonstration. You create safety not by demanding trust, but by living in a way that earns it. You cultivate intimacy not by asking for it, but by going first.

If your wife has to become smaller or muted just to keep the peace, you're not leading her, you're silencing her. You don't earn trust through control, you earn it through consistency. Through follow-through. Through small moments of presence that stack into a foundation of peace. And if your love only shows up when you feel appreciated, it's not love, it's a transaction. Real love isn't a paycheck for being noticed or respected. It's an offering made whether or not it's returned.

THE BATTLEFIELD OF PRESENCE

I've noticed something about the majority of all my favorite stories. There is a leader who steps forward when others retreat. He takes the front line. He gears up when others give up. He sacrifices, even when the cost is high.

In marriage, our battlefield looks different. But the courage required is just as real. The battlefield might be the kitchen, or the nursery at 3am, or in the bedroom where tension is thick and no one is talking. It might be bedtime, when you're tempted to scroll instead of connect. It could be sitting on the couch, looking your wife in the eyes, and saying, "tell me what you're really feeling."

Leadership doesn't mean being loudest in volume. Or confusing your muted expressions as anything other than being cold. It means going first with vulnerability. It means staying present when your instinct is to pull away. It means choosing humility over control. And sometimes, it means giving up your right to be right so peace can have a place in the room.

The immature man says, "That's not my fault, so I shouldn't have to deal with it." **The mature man says,** "That's not my fault, but I'm her husband, so I will hold space for it." This is what presence looks like. Not defensiveness. Not withdrawal. But ownership without blame. Compassion without condition.

While reading this chapter, if you have found yourself thinking, "what about her responsibility? You are not alone. But leadership doesn't wait for fairness. It walks in faithfulness. When you stop your responsibility to focus on accountability, you subsequently say to God, "I don't trust that you are in control in my marriage and I have to get what I'm owed before I continue to do what I am called to."

Chapter 6 will speak directly to your wife's calling. But don't skip ahead. Stay here. Let the Spirit work on you before worrying about her. This chapter is about you. So ask yourself, *If Christ loved the church the way I love my wife, what would the church believe about Him?* What would have Jesus' legacy looked like if he loved the church the way you love your wife? Your love tells a story. Your presence writes the tone of your home.

A LEGACY WORTH LEAVING

For those of you who have kids, they are watching. They're learning what love looks like by how you treat their mom. One day, your daughter may seek a man who treats her the way you treated your wife. Your son may mimic your model of manhood. You're not just shaping your marriage. How you handle conflict is what will shape your legacy. Sacrificial love doesn't just bless your home, it plants seeds for generations. This is more true than I want it to be. I see how my kids are already being influenced by my communication tendencies. And I can see how I've been influenced by my parents communication struggles.

As husbands, You were called to cultivate your wife's flourishing. That means helping her feel safe enough to become who God made her to be.

That might look like:

- Creating safe emotional space so she can rest

- Speaking life over her calling
- Taking responsibility when it would be easier to blame
- Praying for her when she's discouraged
- Listening without fixing
- Building a marriage where dreams are allowed again

This is what sacrificial love looks like. Not flashy. Not perfect. But consistent. Gentle. Strong. Rooted.

Here is what Sacrificial Love Looks Like in Real Life:

• **Show up even when it's inconvenient.** I remember canceling a golf outing to stay home when Kristen was sick. Not because I had to. Because I wanted her to know, she matters more.

• **Speak her value.** One night, I told her, "You are the most important person in this house." She teared up. It wasn't rehearsed. It was real. And it reminded me that our words carry weight.

• **Support her dreams.** When she wanted to pursue a new career, I didn't just say, "Go for it." I made room in our life for her to thrive.

• **Be interruptible.** I turned off the game one night just to hear what was on her heart. That was the moment she felt loved, not later when I finally took care of a request she made earlier in the night.

• **Apologize without deflecting.** I've had to say, "I was wrong," without explaining it away. That's what softens the space between us.

10 TRUTHS EVERY HUSBAND NEEDS TO HEAR

These aren't just truths for your marriage. They're truths for your growth as a man of God. Truths that men need to hear when it comes to identity, insecurity, and conflict in marriage:

1. Your wife is not the enemy, your insecurities are.

Too many men go into fight mode in conflict, seeing their wife as the opposition. But most of the time, the real battle isn't between you and her.

2. Being passive doesn't make you peaceful, it makes you avoidant.

Some men shut down during conflict, thinking "I just don't want to make things worse." But passivity isn't peace, it's avoidance. Ignoring conflict doesn't resolve it; it just lets wounds fester. A man who leads well doesn't avoid hard conversations, he steps into them with wisdom and self-control.

3. You cannot outwork your insecurity.

A lot of men try to achieve their way out of feeling unworthy, working longer hours, making more money, stacking accomplishments. But your worth isn't in what you do, it's in who you are. And if your identity is built on achievements, what happens when you fail? Work on your foundation, not just your success.

4. If your validation comes from your wife's approval, you've given her too much power.

Yes, you should care about what your wife thinks of you. But if your sense of identity rises and falls on whether she's happy with you, you're setting yourself up for emotional instability. Your identity has to be rooted in Christ, not in her moods or expectations. Otherwise, you'll either be a people pleaser or resentful.

5. If you're waiting for your wife to respect you before you love her well, you've already failed.

Too many men withhold love until they feel respected, but leadership isn't conditional. Christ didn't wait for us to deserve His sacrifice. He gave it freely. A husband leads by example, not by demanding what he thinks he deserves. Respect follows a man who lives honorably, not a man who keeps score.

6. Unhealed wounds make you dangerous to the people you love.

If you don't deal with the wounds from your past, your father, your failures, or your fears, you will take them out on the people closest to you. Your anger, withdrawal, criticism, or control issues aren't just personality traits, they are symptoms of something deeper. Your wife shouldn't have to suffer for what you won't heal.

7. Being right in an argument doesn't make you a good leader.

Winning an argument and leading your marriage well are two very different things. If your goal is to prove a point instead of build trust, you might win the battle but lose your wife's heart in the process. A man of wisdom asks himself: *Do I want to be right, or do I want to be close?*

8. You can't demand respect you haven't earned.

Some men expect their wife to automatically trust and respect them, but trust is built, not owed. If you've been inconsistent, unreliable, selfish, or emotionally detached, you can't blame her for not respecting you. You have to earn it back. Stop focusing on what she isn't giving and start focusing on how you can show up better.

9. Your lack of emotional self-control is a leadership failure.

If anger, defensiveness, or shutting down is your default response to conflict, you are letting emotions control you instead of leading from a place of wisdom. Your emotions are real, but they don't get to drive your actions. A strong man can feel his emotions without being ruled by them.

10. A great marriage isn't about finding the perfect wife, it's about becoming the right man.

Some men blame their marriage struggles on what their wife isn't doing instead of looking at how they show up. Your marriage will never outgrow your own spiritual and emotional maturity. If you want a thriving, intimate, and secure marriage, stop asking, *"How can my wife change?"* and start asking, *"How can I grow?"*

CLOSING CHARGE

D. L. Moody once said, *"The world has yet to see what God will do through the man who surrenders everything"* (Moody, *Address at Cambridge, 1883*). His words cut to the core of biblical manhood. A husband's strength is not measured in how much he can control, accomplish, or provide on his own, but in how fully he is yielded to God. Sacrificial love begins where self dies, when a man lays down pride, performance, and posturing, and instead chooses surrender. Identity is not found in ability, but in availability to God.

A surrendered husband becomes the channel through which God's love flows most freely into his wife and family. If you've been waiting on your wife to change so your marriage can get better, this chapter should hit you square in the chest. You were called to go first. Not because you're better, but because that's what love does. Sacrificial love isn't about winning arguments.

It's about winning her heart again and again. But let's be honest: you can't do this on your own. You can't lead her well unless you're being led. So if you're ready to become the husband God called you to be, don't start with more effort. Start with surrender. Let Him lead you. Let Him heal you. Let Him remind you who you are. Because once you know who you are, you'll know how to love.

I've had moments on my knees whispering, "God, I don't know if I can keep showing up like this." Because sacrificial love sounds noble, until it costs something. But here's what I've learned: that kind of love doesn't come from grit. It comes from grace. The more time you spend abiding in Christ, the more capable you become of loving like Him. You don't have to be perfect. But you do have to go first.

Let this chapter be a turning point, not just for your marriage, but for the man you're becoming. And if God really is in control of your marriage, then it doesn't matter if you've been married for 1 year or 50, He can heal what's broken.

Go Deeper With These Verses:

Ephesians 5:25–28, 1 Corinthians 16:13–14, Colossians 3:19, Micah 6:8

APPLICATION FOR HUSBANDS:

Ask yourself:

- Where have I become passive, avoidant, or self-focused in my marriage?
- How would my marriage shift if I led with humility, courage, and consistency?

Then ask your spouse:
"What's one area where you've felt like you're carrying something alone?"

Write down one action you will take this week to shoulder that burden with her, not to fix her, but to stand with her.

APPLICATION FOR WIVES

This week, take a posture of prayer rather than pressure.

Ask your husband: *"What's one area where you feel like you're not measuring up?"* Don't fix. Don't advise. Just listen.

Then, pray for that specific area daily this week. If he's

open to it, speak one sentence of encouragement aloud to him, rooted in what you prayed.

Let your support be a reflection of trust in God, not an attempt to manage your husband's growth.

Husbands Pray This:

Father,

I want to love my wife well, but I often fall short. I let distraction, frustration, or fear lead me instead of Your Spirit.

Teach me how to be present, mentally, emotionally, spiritually. Help me to love like Jesus: not passively, not pridefully, but faithfully.

Remind me that leadership in marriage starts with humility and self-sacrifice. Strengthen my resolve to be the kind of man who brings peace, not pressure.

In Jesus' name, Amen.

Wives Pray This:

Father,

Thank You for the man I am walking through life with. I know You have called him to love with strength and sacrifice, but I also know that calling can feel heavy. Help him to see himself not through the lens of his failures, but through the truth of who You say he is, chosen, equipped, and capable of leading in love.

When he feels inadequate, remind him that Your power

is made perfect in weakness. When he's tempted to withdraw, give him the courage to stay present. When he doubts his role, speak identity into him louder than the voice of shame.

Teach me to encourage without controlling, to support without smothering, and to pray for him more than I criticize him. Show me how to be a safe place for his growth, not his judge, not his coach, but his partner.

Use our marriage to reflect Your love, not because we have it all together, but because You are holding us together.

In Jesus' name, Amen

6

THE WIFE'S CALL: RESPECT THROUGH SUBMISSION

THERE'S PROBABLY no word in modern culture more misunderstood, or more misused in Christian circles, than the word **submission**. It triggers assumptions. It surfaces wounds. And sometimes, it flat-out causes arguments.

But when Paul wrote, *"Wives, submit to your husbands, as to the Lord"* (Ephesians 5:22), he wasn't handing out a chain of command. He was pointing to a divine dance, a posture of strength wrapped in humility. A reflection of how the Church responds to Christ. Not out of fear. Not out of weakness. But because He is trustworthy.

Submission isn't about being silent. It's about being secure. It's not passive. And it's definitely not about enabling control or dysfunction. True submission is voluntary. It's a choice to yield, not because your husband deserves it, but because you trust the One who asked it of you. But here's the reality most people miss: respect and submission are often reactive.

They flow out of safety. Out of trust. They respond to consistent, sacrificial love. A husband who leads with humility and care makes it easier for a wife to respond with honor and respect. That's not weakness, that's wisdom.

Still, some wives have been taught that respect is something you blindly offer no matter what. But God never called women to surrender their voice, their discernment, or their sanity. Submission is not a weapon to be wielded over women. And it is not permission for husbands to act without accountability.

On the contrary, some wives misuse this truth as a justification to withhold respect. They use their husband's failures as permission to shut down, to control, to criticize, or to treat him with disdain. They think, *"If he's not leading well, I don't owe him respect."* But that's not biblical either.

Respect isn't about reward. It's a reflection of your own character, not his. It's easy to honor a man who's earning it daily. But there's something deeply powerful, even redemptive, when a wife chooses to reflect dignity in the face of disappointment. That doesn't mean ignoring real issues or avoiding hard conversations. It means choosing to respond from your identity, not his inadequacy.

When a wife holds respect hostage, hoping her withdrawal will change him, she's not just undermining him, she's forgetting who she is. God doesn't call you to respect your husband because he's perfect. He calls you to respect because you belong to Him, to God. And when your posture reflects the character of Christ, not bitterness, not sarcasm, not control, that's when real influence takes root.

So here's the tension: submission isn't passive. And it isn't blind. But neither is it conditional, manipulative, or withheld as punishment. Withholding respect to teach a lesson isn't strength, it's pride. And pride is the very thing that fractures intimacy and erodes connection.

Yes, if you're married to a man who's not living sacrificially, that's hard, excruciating at times. That deserves honest dialogue, prayer, and real change. But don't let his failure rob you of the opportunity to walk in the fullness of your calling. You can stand firm in truth without stepping out of respect.

THE ILLUSION OF SECURITY

In my previous relationships I've been extremely anxious. I convinced myself that in order to protect a relationship I had to be relentless in pursuing. I didn't realize how jealous, controlling, desperate, and exhausting I had become—not only for the other person, but for myself. I thought constant check-ins, overanalyzing every conversation, and "fixing" every perceived problem would prove my love and secure the relationship.

But deep down, it wasn't love that was driving me. It was fear. Fear of being left. Fear of not being enough. Fear that if I let go for even a moment, the whole thing would fall apart. That fear disguised itself as care, but really it was control.

What I didn't understand at the time was that this kind of relentless grasping doesn't create closeness, it pushes it away. Love can't breathe in an atmosphere of anxiety. Respect can't grow when one person is constantly trying to manage or manipulate the other's emotions and choices.

It took time, distance, a lot of reflection, and honestly several failed relationships to see what was really going on. I wasn't pursuing the other person out of genuine love; I was chasing them to protect my own sense of worth. My identity was tethered to whether or not they stayed. And when your identity is anchored in someone else's behavior, you'll do whatever it takes to keep them, even if it means suffocating them.

True respect in marriage doesn't come from frantic pursuit; it comes from secure love. It's giving space instead of smothering, trusting instead of tracking, supporting instead of suffocating. And that kind of respect only flows when your identity is rooted in something unshakable, when you know who you are in Christ, even if your spouse is having a bad day, or week, or season.

Over time the anxious pursuit and smothering behavior becomes more toxic and damaging. The desperation for security blended with hurt, disappointment, and resentment creates a cocktail of passive aggressive, cold, and contemptuous conflict.

THE COUNTERFEIT: SPIRITUAL PRIDE AND CONTROL

One of the more deceptive pitfalls in marriage, especially for those who take their faith seriously, is the quiet rise of something I'd label as spiritual pride. It often disguises itself as discernment, maturity, or moral concern, but underneath it is a subtle belief: *"I'm more spiritually aware than you are... therefore, I'm justified in how I treat you."*

This posture poisons respect.

It shows up in the form of condescending prayers that sound more like public indictments. It whispers judgments under the veil of "truth-speaking." It uses Scripture as a weapon instead of a light. And perhaps worst of all, you try to hold the position of judge while simultaneously being in the role of victim.

Spiritual pride says, "If you were closer to God, you

wouldn't act like this." But humility says, "Even if you're struggling, I'll still reflect Christ."

A wife walking in spiritual pride may appear devoted on the outside, serving, praying, speaking Scripture. But inwardly, she's fueled by resentment. She begins to treat her husband like her project instead of her partner. And without realizing it, she elevates her own spiritual insight as the standard measuring stick for his worth.

When he doesn't measure up, disrespect creeps in. Emotional withdrawal is justified. She alienates others from him in the name of "righteous boundaries." But here's the truth: God never called wives to be the Holy Spirit in their husband's life.

Your job is not to convict. Your job is to reflect Christ, even when your husband doesn't. That doesn't mean ignoring sin or tolerating abuse. But it does mean refusing to weaponize faith to elevate yourself or shame your spouse.

Spiritual pride is just pride, dressed in religious clothing. When pride is a mask, it hides a person's deep fear that they are not enough, not in control, or not truly loved. So instead of being vulnerable, they protect themselves with spiritual lingo, blame, or rigid black-and-white thinking. Pride thrives when we are too afraid to be wrong, too insecure to be vulnerable, and too convinced we must stay in control. And pride always separates. It separates a wife from her husband. It separates her from intimacy with God. And it separates her from the humility required to grow.

If you're always the spiritually "right" one in the marriage, then you're probably not growing. Because the woman God uses most powerfully is not the one who's always right, it's the one who stays humble, tender, and teachable.

You can pray constantly, quote Scripture daily, and still walk in pride. You can appear spiritual and still miss the heart of Jesus. When submission becomes about control, when respect is demanded but never returned, when spiritual language is used to shame, manipulate, or guilt, that's not biblical womanhood. That's fear cloaked in righteousness.

Here are a few warning signs that respect has been replaced by pride or control:

- **Martyrdom and over-sacrifice**: Giving endlessly but resenting it internally. Often rooted in a need to feel morally superior.
- **Spiritual manipulation**: Phrases like "If you really loved God..." are often about shame, not love.
- **Moral victimhood**: Always praying for your spouse to change, while ignoring your own part in the tension.
- **Relational isolation**: Demanding others pick sides or withdrawing from community to maintain control.
- **Eternal judgment in conflict**: Demonizing your spouse or threatening hell in the middle of a disagreement is spiritual abuse, not conviction.

God never asked you to be your husband's savior. He asked you to be his partner. When your posture reflects Christ, not control, your influence becomes powerful, even healing.

WHAT SUBMISSIVE RESPECT IS

So let's rebuild the truth of what biblical respect actually looks like. True submissive respect is rooted in a deep **trust in God**, not in the behavior or performance of your husband. Submission is not about being small. It's about being strong enough to yield without losing your voice. It's a posture of confidence, not cowardice.

Here are five practical ways wives can cultivate and communicate respect in their marriage, not just as a feeling, but as a daily rhythm. Respect in marriage often looks like:

1. **Speaking with honor, even when you're frustrated:** The goal isn't to bottle your emotions. It's to express them in a way that preserves connection. Try: *"I'm struggling to feel seen right now, but I still believe in you."* That kind of honesty disarms defensiveness and builds trust.

2. **Protect his reputation in public:** Disrespect often starts subtly, an eye-roll, a jab, a story told at his expense. But public honor is a form of private love. It tells your husband: *"I've got your back, even when no one's looking."*

3. **Encourage His Leadership Without Mocking His Mistakes:** Even if your husband fumbles, your encouragement has the power to reinforce his growth. A gentle "thank you for trying" goes further than a sarcastic "well that didn't work."

4. **Responding rather than reacting:** Reactions are automatic. Responses are intentional. When he misses the mark, take a breath before you

reply. Ask yourself: *"Am I responding from my identity, or my insecurity?"*

5. **Pray with Him, Not Just for Him:** Praying for your husband is powerful. But praying with your husband is intimate. It's an act of mutual submission. It breaks down barriers. And it reminds both of you that this isn't a power struggle, it's a partnership.

And sometimes, submission is choosing silence, not to be passive, but to protect peace. Respect and submission don't mean you abandon discernment. They don't mean you tolerate abuse or accept sin. **Biblical submission always has boundaries, because God values your wholeness.**

A WORD TO THE WIFE WRESTLING WITH THIS

Maybe your husband hasn't been worthy of respect lately. Maybe you feel alone in carrying the spiritual weight. Maybe your efforts are met with indifference. Maybe you've tried to show respect, and it hasn't changed anything. You're not called to pretend. You're called to be faithful. You're called to respond to God first.

Submission is not blind obedience, it's strategic trust.

It says: *"God, I trust You more than I trust this situation."*

It says: *"I'll speak truth in love, but I won't abandon the posture of peace."*

It says: *"Even if he doesn't see who he is, I won't lose sight of who I am."*

And that's where it starts, knowing your true identity. You are not weak. You are not invisible. You are not responsible for your husband's salvation or maturity. You are a daughter of the King

And when you live from that place, you don't have to control or manipulate, you simply reflect the heart of God in your words, your posture, and your peace.

7 HARD TRUTHS WIVES NEED TO HEAR

These are not attacks, they're invitations. Invitations to reflect, reset, and return to the kind of strength that flows from secure identity.

1. If you have to control everything, you don't trust anyone, including God.

Control is not leadership. It's fear with a steering wheel. And often, the need to control your husband is rooted in a deeper fear that God won't take care of you.

2. Criticism doesn't change a man's heart, respect does.

Most husbands aren't hardened by their wife's honesty. They're hardened by the contempt that often comes with it. Your tone can shut a man down before your words even land.

3. Spiritual superiority makes intimacy impossible.

If you position yourself as the "more mature" one in every conversation, don't be surprised when your husband pulls away. No one feels safe opening up to someone who sees themselves as above correction.

4. Your frustration is valid, but how you express it determines whether your home heals or fractures.

Your emotions matter. But unresolved disappointment

often becomes sarcasm, shame, or silence. That's not strength. That's a slow drip of disconnection.

5. Disrespect never builds the respect you're craving.

Withholding warmth, belittling his efforts, or mocking his leadership doesn't motivate, it demoralizes. If you want him to grow into his role, stop pushing him out of it.

6. Telling your friends everything your husband does wrong isn't venting, it's betrayal.

There's a difference between seeking godly counsel and poisoning the well of your marriage. Respect begins when you protect what's sacred, even in disappointment.

7. You don't have to feel respect to give it.

Respect is not a reward for performance. It's a reflection of who *you* are. And when you choose to give it, even when it's undeserved, you invite something deeper than agreement. You invite transformation.

CLOSING CHARGE

You don't have to be a silent woman to be a submissive one. You don't have to shrink yourself to be strong in Christ. And you don't have to agree with everything your husband says to still honor who God called him to be.

Submission isn't about disappearing. It's about displaying something bigger than yourself, something sacred. It's about choosing a posture that says: "I trust God enough to yield even when I don't feel in control." It's about loving with courage, respecting with conviction, and walking with the kind of grace that only comes from knowing who you are in Christ.

The legacy you build doesn't come from how perfect your husband becomes. It comes from how faithfully you reflect Christ in the in-between. And sometimes, the most powerful thing a wife can do is to respond with peace when chaos would be easier. To choose dignity when disrespect is easier. To speak life when bitterness is on the tip of her tongue.

This is not a call to tolerate sin, abuse, or silence your voice. This is a call to take your place as a woman of strength and humility. To submit, not because your husband earned it, but because your Savior did.

So here's the question:
If your respect was the only picture your husband
had of God's character, what would he believe
about Him?

Let that question shape not just how you speak, but who you're becoming. You are not invisible. You are not voiceless. You are not powerless. You are inherently valuable. And that makes you a force of peace, wisdom, and strength in your home.

Respecting your husband is foundational to a healthy and thriving marriage. The Bible, particularly in Ephesians 5:33, emphasizes the importance of a wife showing respect to her husband. This respect can manifest in many practical ways, fostering love, trust, and unity within the marriage.

Here are five ways to show respect to your husband:

1. **Listen Actively and Value His Opinions**: One of the most powerful ways to respect your husband is to listen to him actively. This means giving him your full attention when he speaks, valuing his thoughts, ideas, and opinions,

even if they differ from your own. Acknowledging his perspective shows that you respect his intellect and insights.

2. **Support His Leadership and Decisions**: While marriage is a partnership where decisions should be made together, supporting your husband's leadership role, particularly in areas where he takes the initiative, is a way to show respect. This doesn't mean blindly agreeing with everything, but rather trusting his judgment and showing confidence in his ability to lead, while also providing your input in a loving and constructive manner.

3. **Speak Kindly and Avoid Criticism**: The words you choose can significantly impact how respected your husband feels. Speaking kindly and avoiding unnecessary criticism, especially in front of others, helps to build him up. When you need to address issues, do so privately and with a tone of love and concern, rather than frustration or anger.

4. **Show Appreciation and Gratitude**: Regularly expressing appreciation for the things your husband does, whether big or small, reinforces that you notice and value his efforts. Simple acts of gratitude, such as thanking him for his hard work or acknowledging the ways he supports the family, can go a long way in showing respect.

5. **Trust and Honor His Intentions**: Trusting your husband means believing that he has your best interests at heart and honoring his intentions, even if things don't always go as planned. Avoid assuming the worst or questioning his motives without cause. Instead, give him the benefit of the doubt and communicate openly about any concerns you may have.

Respect in marriage isn't just about what you do, but also about the attitude with which you do it. By consistently showing respect in these ways, you're not only honoring your husband, but also nurturing a marriage that reflects the love and unity that God intended.

Here are few things to remember as we move forward in the book and discuss how we can practically overcome insecurities in our marriage.

1. **Words Have Power**: Proverbs 18:21 states, "The tongue has the power of life and death." This verse reminds us that our words can either build someone up or tear them down. Speaking kindly fosters a positive environment where love and encouragement thrive, whereas harsh words can cause deep wounds, creating division and resentment in the relationship.

2. **Foster a Safe Emotional Environment**: A marriage should be a safe haven where both partners feel valued, loved, and respected. When you speak kindly to your spouse, you contribute to an environment where he feels emotionally secure. Over time, constant criticism can erode self-esteem and trust, making it difficult for him to open up or be vulnerable with you.

3. **Promote Healthy Communication**: Kindness in speech facilitates healthy, open communication. When you speak kindly, it invites your spouse to listen and engage in the conversation, knowing that your intentions are rooted in love and respect.

4. **Reflecting Christ's Love**: As Christians, we are called to reflect Christ's love in our relationships. Ephesians 4:29 advises, "Do not let any unwholesome talk come out of your mouths, but only what is helpful for building others up according to their needs, that it may benefit those who listen." Speaking kindly mirrors the love and grace that Christ extends to us.

5. **Encouraging Growth and Positive Change**: Constructive feedback, when delivered kindly, can encourage growth and positive change. Criticism, however, often comes across as judgmental or condemning, which can make your husband feel discouraged or unappreciated.

Speaking kindly and avoiding criticism is important because it nurtures love, trust, and emotional safety in your marriage. It aligns with biblical teachings on the power of words and the call to build each other up in love. By choosing kindness, you contribute to a marriage that reflects the grace and compassion that God desires for us.

————

Go Deeper With These Verses

1 Peter 3:1–4, Proverbs 31:25–26, Titus 2:3–5, Philippians 2:3–5

————

APPLICATION FOR WIVES

Ask yourself:

• When am I most tempted to control, criticize, or correct?

• What fear is underneath that tendency?

Then take one area of tension and pray:

"Lord, help me trade control for trust. Show me what it looks like to encourage rather than critique in this area."

Choose one specific way this week to affirm your husband's efforts, even if they're imperfect.

APPLICATION FOR HUSBANDS

This week, don't focus on fixing her behaviors, focus on connecting with her heart.

• Ask your wife: *"What's one thing you're carrying emotionally that I haven't really asked about?"* Listen without interrupting or problem-solving. Affirm her strength out loud. Tell her something specific you see in her that reflects Christ.

Let your presence speak louder than your plans. Reflect love, not pressure.

————

Wives Pray This:

Lord,

You know the weight I carry in this relationship. Sometimes I feel unseen, unheard, or under-appreciated. But I know You see me.

Teach me how to respect with strength. Show me how to use my voice without trying to control. Help me reflect Your character more than I reflect my fear.

I want to be a woman who builds, not breaks. A woman who uplifts, not undermines. A woman rooted in You, not driven by insecurity.

In Jesus' name, Amen.

Husbands Pray This:

Father,

Thank You for the woman You've entrusted to walk beside me. I know You've designed her with strength, beauty, and insight that reflects Your heart. Help her believe that, not just on good days, but especially when insecurity creeps in.

When she feels overlooked, remind her that You see. When she wrestles with her worth, speak truth into the places where old wounds still whisper.

Show me how to love her in ways that quiet fear and build trust. Teach me to lead with gentleness, not pride. To protect without controlling. To pursue her heart, not just her habits.

Give me the wisdom to create space for her voice and the humility to listen. Make me the kind of man who reflects the love of Christ in our home.

In Jesus' name, Amen.

7

OVERCOMING INSECURITIES IN MARRIAGE

PARENTING a toddler is both a beautiful blessing and one of life's most humbling challenges. I'm convinced the inspiration for Jekyll and Hyde must have come from observing a toddler. One moment, my son is sweet and affectionate, melting my heart with an unprompted "I love you so much, Daddy." The next, I'm being smacked on the face and told, "I'll whack you away, Daddy!" It's a rollercoaster of emotions that's as exhausting as it is rewarding. And yet, through all the chaos, I've realized that some of life's most profound lessons about relationships and identity are right in front of me, in his tiny body and big feelings.

One particular lesson came during a stretch of night when he developed a fascination and fear of bears. He was completely intrigued by them. He loved books about bears, talked about them constantly, and pretended to be one in his playtime growls. But at night, when the lights went out, bears became the monster under the bed, or in his case, in his room.

Every bedtime for a while, he would ask me and Kristen,

"Are there bears in my room?" At first, I responded the way most logical adults would: I tried to reason with him.

"There are no bears in your room, buddy. Bears live in the forest or the zoo." I would try to calmly explain how ridiculous the idea of a bear in his room was. He'd seem to accept my explanation for the moment, but the next night, we were right back to the same question: "Are there bears in my room?"

It was frustrating at first, and then it hit me: reasoning wasn't what my son needed. He wasn't asking me to teach him about the habitats of bears or the impossibility of one being in his room. He needed comfort. He needed reassurance. He needed to feel safe, not be reasoned with. So I changed my approach.

"Are there bears in my room?" he asked again.

I crouched down to his eye level, held his tiny hand, and replied, "Bears? Buddy, Daddy's here. No matter what, I'll be here to keep you safe."

He hesitated for a moment like the wheels were turning in his brain, and then asked, "And Mommy protect me too?"

"Absolutely," I said, smiling. "Mommy and I will always love you and protect you, especially from bears." And just like that, the fear began to fade, not because it stopped existing, but because he stopped facing it alone.

This seemingly small interaction opened my eyes to a bigger truth about relationships. How many times have I responded with a solution instead of presence? It's instinctive. We want to fix, but sometimes, fear and insecurity aren't asking to be solved. They're asking to be seen.

When someone you love says, "I don't know if I can do this," they're not asking for a motivational speech. They're asking, "Will you still love me if I'm scared?" When they say,

"I'm feeling overwhelmed," what they often need is not a three-step plan, but a hand to hold.

What my toddler taught me is this: logic doesn't always address the emotional need. Fear, insecurity, and doubt aren't always rational, but they're always real to the person experiencing them. Validation isn't about agreeing with the fear or solving the problem, it's about saying, "I see you. I hear you. You're not alone."

In relationships, just like with my son's bedtime worries, comfort builds trust. And trust is the foundation of a secure relationship. My son didn't stop fearing bears because I convinced him they couldn't exist in his room. He didn't stop fearing them because they weren't real. He stopped fearing them because he didn't feel alone.

This principle is evident all throughout Scripture. Isaiah declares, "So do not fear, for I am with you" (Isa. 41:10). Moses tells Israel, "Be strong and courageous. Do not fear... for it is the Lord your God who goes with you (Deut. 31:6). And God Himself reminds Joshua multiple times, "Be strong and courageous...for the Lord your God will be with you wherever you go" (Josh. 1:9).

That's the kind of reassurance we all crave. We want to know that when we voice our fears, no matter how irrational they might seem, someone will say, "I'm here for you. I've got your back." Caring for a spouse who's battling insecurities means stepping into their emotional world, not with answers, but with empathy. We respond in a way that provides comfort in the face of fear. For my son, it was being a protector of what he was afraid of, bears.

Here are the four steps to be a "Bear Protector" aka a "C.A.R.E Bear"

C – Connect

Connection begins when you choose to be fully present. This means setting aside distractions, whether it's your phone, the TV, or even your own thoughts about how to fix the problem. Your partner doesn't need solutions right away, they need your attention.

How to Do It:

- Make eye contact, nod occasionally, and offer verbal cues like "I'm listening" or "Go on."
- Avoid jumping in with advice or dismissing their feelings with phrases like, "That's nothing to worry about" or "You're overthinking it." And avoid the conversation killers like, "That's not true!", "That's not what I said." Or "That's not what really happened."
- Ask open-ended questions like, "Can you tell me more about what's on your mind?" to encourage them to share fully.

By listening without judgment, you send the message: *You matter, and I'm here for you.*

A – Acknowledge

Validation is the cornerstone of emotional safety. Acknowledge what your partner is feeling, even if it seems irrational or exaggerated to you. Accepting their emotions doesn't mean you have to agree with them; it means recognizing their experience as real and valid. The message you are sending is that your partner matters more to you than being right.

How to Do It:

- Use phrases like, "That sounds really overwhelming," or "I can see why you'd feel that way."
- Avoid trying to "correct" their emotions with logic or minimizing their feelings by saying, "It's not a big deal."
- Reflect back what they're expressing: "It seems like you're feeling really stressed about this situation."

When you acknowledge and accept their emotions, you're saying: *I see you, and I'm not going to dismiss what you're going through.*

R – Reassure

Reassurance isn't about fixing the problem; it's about being a steady presence in the storm. Your partner needs to know they're not alone, that you're in their corner no matter what. Reassurance calms the emotional "fight or flight" response and creates a sense of stability.

How to Do It:

- Offer simple, steady words like, "I'm here," or "We'll figure this out together."
- If appropriate, use physical reassurance, holding their hand, offering a hug, or sitting close to them.
- Reiterate your commitment: "You don't have to face this alone. I'm with you every step of the way." Or "I'm on your team."

Reassurance builds trust and sends the message: *You're safe with me, no matter what.*

E – Engage

Words of comfort are essential, but they need to be backed up by consistent actions. Engagement shows your partner that you're not just saying the right things; you're actively supporting them. This step reinforces your commitment and builds long-term trust.

How to Do It:

- If your partner expresses a specific need, follow through on it. For example, if they're overwhelmed, offer to take something off their plate.
- Take initiative. Don't wait for them to ask for help; look for ways to make their day easier or more manageable.
- Engage in small but meaningful ways: leave a note of encouragement, cook their favorite meal,

or simply sit with them in silence when words aren't enough.

Engagement communicates: *You can count on me to show up, not just talk about it.*

PUTTING IT ALL TOGETHER

The **CARE** framework creates a roadmap for being present and supportive in moments of vulnerability. Whether your partner is dealing with fears, insecurities, or everyday stresses, these steps help build a foundation of trust, safety, and emotional security. By practicing **CARE**, you're not only offering comfort in the moment but also strengthening your relationship for the long haul.

Being a "Bear Protector" isn't about perfection, it's about showing up with intention and love, time and time again.

INSECURITY AND IDENTITY

Here's the hard truth: identity issues don't always look like insecurity. Sometimes it shows up as anger. Sometimes control. Sometimes avoidance. But underneath it all is the same ache: *Do I matter? Am I safe? Can I trust that I'm enough?*

When identity is rooted in Christ, we love from security, not desperation. But when we forget who we are, we start trying to earn what we already have. That's when insecurity creeps in. And when your spouse is the one struggling, your job is not to fix them. It's to reflect the Father's love. It's like sending up a flare to help them navigate back to the security of their true identity.

That means you speak life when they feel like a burden. You stay steady when their emotions swing. You offer grace when they expect rejection. That's what God does for us. And it's what He invites us to do for each other.

And even if you *try* to fix your spouse, it won't work. At least not in the way you hope. You might have the right intentions, the right words, even the right advice. But when someone feels insecure, they don't need a solution, they need security. They need to know that their brokenness doesn't make them unlovable. They need to see that their spouse can handle their mess without pulling away.

Fixing says, *"You need to change so I can feel okay."*

Love says, *"Even if nothing changes, I'm not going anywhere."*

I've seen it in my own marriage, and with countless couples in counseling: the more we push to correct, the more our partner feels criticized. The more we offer solutions, the more they feel like a problem. And when someone already feels like a burden, even your "help" can feel like pressure.

But when you stop fixing and start *seeing,* when you stop correcting and start *caring,* that's when healing begins. Because love doesn't say, *"I'll be close when you're better."* It says, *"I'm with you while it's hard."* This restores confidence, reaffirms identity, and slowly dissolves insecurity from the inside out.

WHAT INSECURITY MIGHT LOOK LIKE IN YOUR MARRIAGE

Sometimes insecurity is easier to recognize in others than in ourselves. It doesn't always look like fear, it often wears a disguise. It might look like criticism: "Why don't you ever hug me anymore?" Or silence: "Nothing's wrong," even when something clearly is. Or micromanaging: "Don't forget to say this. And make sure you do that." Or sarcasm that cuts just a little too deep.

Beneath those reactions is the same vulnerable question: *Can I trust you to care about what I feel?*

There are times in conflict with my wife when I feel a quiet tug inside me, like a small voice saying, "You're not handling this well." It's humbling because I know better, but the stubbornness in me wants to win the argument or prove my point. I feel justified in the moment, but afterward, the guilt is immediate.

Instead of owning it, I often find ways to blame her, convincing myself that my guilt is her fault, not mine. It's a cycle of pride that turns confession into deflection. It's such a clear picture of how false identity shows up in conflict, how insecurity can turn a moment that should be about restoration into a power struggle.

What I'm learning is that the voice of identity never sounds like blame. It sounds like invitation: to drop the weapons, to own my part, and to lead from security, not from fear.

LET'S BRING IT INTO REAL-LIFE SCENARIOS:

Sarah feels invisible. Her husband, Jason, thinks everything is fine because she hasn't said otherwise. But her silence isn't peace, it's resignation. When she finally speaks up and says, "I don't feel like I matter to you," he responds with logic: "That's not true," and walks away.

What would CARE look like? Jason could say, "I didn't

realize I was coming across that way. Help me understand what you're feeling. I want to do better."

In another relationship, Marcus emotionally shuts down during conflict. His wife, Rachel, accuses him of being cold. What she doesn't know is that Marcus was raised in a home where emotions were mocked. Vulnerability feels dangerous, not natural.

What would CARE look like? Rachel could say, "I know this isn't easy for you. You don't have to get it perfect, I just want to understand you better. I'm here when you're ready."

These examples remind us: insecurity doesn't always show up waving a red flag. Sometimes it whispers through distance or lashes out in frustration. The key isn't to take those moments personally, it's to become curious about what's underneath.

And when you learn to see what's *beneath* the reaction, you can meet your spouse with compassion instead of defensiveness. That's the beginning of emotional safety, and the beginning of healing.

RECOGNIZING THE ROOTS OF INSECURITY

Insecurity doesn't come out of nowhere. It has a history. A story. A root system that's often buried deep beneath the surface.

Maybe your spouse had a parent who only noticed mistakes. Maybe they were cheated on in a past relationship and now feel panic when they see you on your phone. Maybe you were raised in a home where emotions were unsafe, and now conflict makes you want to shut down or leave the room.

These reactions don't always *look* like insecurity. They

look like control. Or distance. Or defensiveness. But underneath, they're all asking the same thing: *Am I safe here?*

You can't heal what you won't name. And you can't name what you won't face.

That's why healing insecurity in marriage begins by slowing down and asking:

- Where did this start?
- Why does this fear feel so familiar?
- What am I trying to protect myself from?
- What would it cost me to let go of control?

These questions don't always have immediate answers. Sometimes the roots are subtle, like a father who never said "I'm proud of you," or a family culture where emotions were never discussed. Those experiences teach powerful messages: *Don't be a burden. Keep it together. Don't show weakness.*

Other times, the roots are more obvious: betrayal, abandonment, infidelity, or years of feeling alone in your own marriage. These wounds don't disappear on their own. They calcify into survival strategies, ways of relating that feel safe, even if they push intimacy away.

But here's the hope: you are not bound by your history. The past explains the wound, but it doesn't get to write the ending. This is why I've said in order to not be lost in a false identity we need to know where we are and where we are going. Answering these questions are part of locating yourself in the dense woods and begin the restorative process.

Insecurity may have taken root in your childhood or past relationships, but it doesn't have to define your future. Not when healing is possible. Not when Christ is your foundation. Not when love is stronger than fear.

THE IMPACT OF INSECURITIES ON MARRIAGE

Insecurity doesn't stay isolated. It seeps into how you hear each other, respond to each other, and even how you interpret silence. It reshapes the emotional tone of the entire relationship.

When you carry insecurity into marriage, it turns small moments into confirmation of a deeper fear: *I'm not enough. I'm not wanted. I don't matter.*

A missed hug becomes proof of rejection. A delayed text feels like abandonment. A gentle critique sounds like, *You're a failure.*

And then the cycle begins.

One partner feels inadequate, so they seek reassurance. The other feels pressured and pulls away. That distance reinforces the original fear. Both partners feel misunderstood. One feels invisible. The other feels accused. Instead of reaching for each other, they retreat behind defense mechanisms.

Insecurity doesn't just affect what you *feel*. It affects how you *act*. Some spouses try to control everything, believing safety depends on keeping order. Others shut down, avoiding the risk of vulnerability. Some turn every disagreement into a test: *If you loved me, you'd already know what I need.* Others stop asking for anything, convinced they don't deserve it.

And slowly, the lines between insecurity and identity start to blur.

This is just who I am, we tell ourselves. But it's not. It's who you became to feel safe. It's a response. A survival strategy. It's not your true self.

When you understand that truth, you stop reacting to symptoms and start responding to the heart. You stop expecting perfection and start cultivating safety. You stop trying to fix your spouse and start helping them feel safe enough to grow.

That's what transforms a marriage, not advice, not lectures, not criticism. Safety. Love. Presence. And validation is a great practical tool that we can use in our communication to cultivate that safety.

Validation is about receiving what your spouse shares, no matter how clumsy or intense, and showing them it matters. It's not about agreeing with everything they say. It's about catching what they're tossing you with care.

EGG-TOSS ANALOGY

Have you ever played the game egg-toss? The summer camp game where you toss the egg back and forth and try to not break it? Imagine your spouse's emotions as an egg. Sometimes they toss it gently. Other times, it's hurled at you, loaded with frustration, fear, or pain.

If they've been let down in the past, they might expect you to drop it or smash it. Their history says: no one ever catches it.

But your role isn't to fix how they toss the egg. It's to catch it, carefully, without dropping it, even if it's coming in hot.

Each time you catch it gently, you're telling them:

"You don't have to throw so hard. I'm not going to drop it."

"You don't have to test me. I'm not them."

"You're safe with me."

But if you put up a wall or dismiss their feelings, it's the same as letting the egg shatter. Even if your intentions are different, the result feels the same to them: another broken egg.

Validation doesn't mean agreeing with everything. It means being the safe place where they can be seen, where their fears don't have to be their identity anymore.

Validation, like catching an egg with care, builds trust and teaches your spouse it's okay to be vulnerable. It says, "I'm with you. I can handle your mess. I'm not going to let it break us."

REFRAMING INSECURITY THROUGH TRUE IDENTITY

If insecurity is the wound, identity in Christ is the healing. You can't outperform insecurity. You can't out-argue it or bury it in self-help. And no matter how much your spouse reassures you, it will never be enough if your identity is still tied to your fear. Insecurity has to be replaced. And only identity in Christ is strong enough to do that.

That's why this book keeps circling back to identity, because until you know who you are in Christ, you'll keep looking to your spouse to tell you. And they were never meant to carry that weight.

Scripture says:

- You are fearfully and wonderfully made (Psalm 139:14)
- You are a new creation in Christ (2 Corinthians 5:17)

- You are chosen, holy, and dearly loved
  (Colossians 3:12)

That's not a motivational poster. It's a foundation.

When you forget who you are, your spouse's tone can ruin your whole day. Their silence becomes shame. Their frustration becomes failure. But when your identity is secure, you're not walking on eggshells hoping for approval. You can stay grounded, even when emotions are high.

Identity shifts your posture in marriage. You stop reacting. You start responding. You stop defending. You start listening. You stop trying to earn love. You start offering it.

And when your spouse is the one struggling? You won't try to talk them out of their fear or dismiss their insecurity. You'll be steady, because your peace isn't dependent on their mood.

You don't have to be perfect. But you do need to be anchored. Because the more secure you are in your identity, the less power insecurity has to run your relationship.

CULTIVATING EMOTIONAL SAFETY IN MARRIAGE

Security in marriage doesn't come from having all the answers. It comes from knowing that when things get hard, your partner won't turn away.

That's emotional safety.

It's not the absence of conflict. It's not pretending everything is fine. It's the quiet confidence that, even in the mess, you're not alone. Your spouse is still with you. Still listening. Still choosing you.

And you don't build that kind of safety with words alone. You build it through consistency, through how you respond when things are tense, through your tone in everyday moments, and through your willingness to stay engaged when emotions run high.

Here's what that looks like in real time:

- When your spouse shares something vulnerable, don't jump in to fix or defend. Stay present. Take a breath. Remind yourself: this isn't about solving the problem, it's about holding space for it.
- Keep your body language open. Don't fold your arms or sigh with frustration. Show them with your posture that they're not a burden.
- Affirm what they're feeling, even if you don't agree with how it's showing up. Say things like, "I didn't realize that was weighing on you," or "Thanks for trusting me with that."

Sarcasm shuts down safety. So does turning vulnerability into a debate. When someone opens their heart, they aren't looking for a rebuttal, they're looking for reassurance.

This doesn't mean you avoid truth. But truth without tenderness feels like an attack. And you'll never get honesty from someone who believes their honesty will be used against them. Couples who create emotional safety don't need to win arguments. They just need to win trust.

Here are a few ways to build that trust:

- **Create a "safe zone" for hard conversations.** Carve out time weekly where each of you can

share what's been on your heart without
interruption, correction, or critique.

- **Use "I" statements instead of accusations.** "I
  felt dismissed when..." will get you further than
  "You never care about..."
- **Stay emotionally consistent.** If your spouse
  opens up and is met with mockery or distance,
  they'll stop opening up. But if they're met with
  steady presence, they'll learn they're safe
  with you.

Your marriage will only go as deep as the safety you
create. So if you want deeper intimacy, start by becoming
the kind of spouse who can hold emotion without fear and
speak truth without harm.

MORE PRACTICAL TOOLS FOR OVERCOMING INSECURITY TOGETHER

Insecurity doesn't automatically vanish just because you
name it. Healing takes work, intentional, often uncomfortable, but deeply rewarding work. And while no spouse can
do that work for the other, they *can* walk beside them in it.

Here are five practical ways to support each other in the
process:

1. Speak Daily Affirmations Over Each Other

Words shape beliefs. When you consistently speak life
into your spouse's identity, you help rewrite the old narratives they've internalized, especially if those messages were
critical or conditional growing up.

Start simple. Say something honest and grounded in love:

- "You are enough, even when today is hard."
- "I see how you show up for our family. I'm thankful for you."
- "You're not failing. You're growing. And I'm proud of you."

2. Journal Your Fears, Then Write God's Truth Over Them

Insecurity often speaks in lies: "I'm too much," "I'm not good enough," "I'm a burden." Combat those lies with truth from Scripture. Try this simple exercise:

1. Write down the lie.
2. Underneath it, write a verse that speaks truth.
3. Then finish with a short personal reminder.

Example:

Lie: "I'll never be enough."
Truth: "You are God's masterpiece" (Ephesians 2:10).
Reminder: "I am chosen, known, and secure in Christ."
Do this together or individually, and revisit it often.

3. Create a Weekly Heart Check-In

Set aside 10–15 minutes once a week to ask questions that foster emotional connection:

- "What's something you felt this week that I might have missed?"
- "When did you feel loved or supported by me?"
- "Is there anything I can do differently next week?"

This isn't a performance review. It's about staying emotionally attuned. You're not fixing each other. You're showing up.

4. Practice Intentional Gratitude

Gratitude is one of the most overlooked tools in healing insecurity. It shifts your focus from lack to appreciation, from resentment to connection. Say thank you for the little things:

- "Thank you for making that call, it meant a lot."
- "I noticed how patient you were earlier. That really helped me feel calm."
- "I'm grateful for your steady presence today."

Gratitude builds emotional safety, softens tension, and reminds your spouse that they're seen.

5. Pick One Way to Lighten Each Other's Load This Week

Ask: *"What's one thing I can take off your plate this week?"* Sometimes insecurity is fueled by overwhelmed feelings. Showing up in small, sacrificial ways helps shoulder the weight and communicates: *"We're in this together."*

Whether it's running an errand, handling bedtime, or

taking initiative with chores, these actions speak love in ways that words sometimes can't.

THE ROLE OF FORGIVENESS IN HEALING INSECURITIES

Unhealed pain is fertile ground for insecurity. A sharp comment that never got resolved. A broken promise that was never acknowledged. A deeper betrayal that still hasn't been named. When those wounds remain buried, they don't disappear. They fester. They grow into defensiveness, withdrawal, criticism, or overcompensation. And over time, they corrode connection.

That's why forgiveness isn't just a spiritual command, it's a relational necessity. Without it, insecurity festers. With it, the heart begins to breathe again.

But let's be clear: forgiveness and trust are not the same.

- Forgiveness is a gift you offer freely.
- Trust is something that gets rebuilt over time.

Forgiveness says, *"I won't hold this against you."*

Trust says, *"I'm watching how you handle my heart going forward."*

If you're the one who's been hurt, forgiveness doesn't mean pretending the wound didn't matter. It means refusing to be shaped by it. It's a declaration: *"This won't define me. This won't define us. I'm choosing to release what could have hardened me."*

If you're the one who did the hurting, forgiveness isn't a license to move on as if nothing happened. You can't demand healing just because you said "I'm sorry." Consistency matters. Humility matters. Showing up with gentleness over time helps your spouse feel safe again, but only if your actions align with your apology.

One couple I worked with had years of hidden resentment between them. There was no blow-up moment, just quiet bitterness, long silences, and lingering mistrust. When they finally named the hurt and grieved it together, it was like oxygen entered the room for the first time in years. Forgiveness didn't erase the pain, but it opened the door to healing. It gave them a place to begin again.

That's what forgiveness does. It breaks the grip of bitterness. It softens hard hearts. It clears the static. It doesn't make the past disappear, but it gives the future a real chance to grow.

Isn't that what Jesus does for us? He meets us in our mess, not with shame, but with grace. Not with cold distance, but with undeserved closeness. When we reflect that kind of mercy in our marriage, we create space for redemption to take root.

BUILDING A VISION OF SECURITY IN MARRIAGE

Healing insecurity isn't just about pulling weeds. It's about planting something better in their place. If you want to build a secure marriage, you need a vision for what that looks like. You need to know what you're aiming for.

So imagine this:

A marriage where love doesn't have to be earned. Where trust isn't constantly in question. Where both people can be fully known and still fully chosen.

That's the power of identity-rooted love. You're not performing. You're not competing. You're not keeping score.

You're resting in the truth that you're already loved, by God and by each other.

In a secure marriage you don't need to fix each other. You walk with each other. You can confess weakness without fear of rejection. You can celebrate each other's strengths without feeling small. You can handle hard conversations without spiraling into self-doubt. You can show up, confident that love will still be there at the end of the day.

When emotional safety is present, love doesn't have to shout to be heard. It doesn't posture or manipulate. It doesn't twist or retreat. It shows up consistently, humbly, and generously.

This is the kind of marriage God designed. Not one without hardship, but one where hardship doesn't win. A marriage where each person is rooted enough in Christ to stay steady through the storms.

And if that feels out of reach right now, start small:

- Choose connection over control.
- Speak truth over fear.
- Hold space instead of defending yourself.
- Ask God to shape your tone, not just your words.

Because when both spouses begin living from identity instead of insecurity, the whole atmosphere of the relationship changes. Fear loosens its grip. Trust grows stronger. And love becomes more than a feeling, it becomes a foundation.

CLOSING CHARGE

You don't have to be the solution to your spouse's insecurity. You just have to be their steady place.

Insecurity isn't healed by lectures or logic. It's softened by love. Dissolved by consistency. Healed through presence. Your job isn't to fix their fears, it's to reflect the Father's heart in the middle of them.

So here's the challenge: Stop trying to reason your spouse out of their pain. Sit with them in it. Reassure them they're not alone. Choose connection when everything in you wants to defend, withdraw, or explain it away.

Because in the end, it's not your arguments that build safety. It's your presence. It's your tone. It's your willingness to say, "I'm not going anywhere, even when this feels messy."

You don't have to be a perfect spouse. But you do need to be a present one. Insecurity loses its grip when love shows up, over and over again. When comfort replaces criticism. When empathy takes the place of evaluation. When connection becomes more important than control.

Be a "Bear Protector." Calm the fear with quiet strength. Hold steady in the storm. Lead with Christlike care. Because in the end, it's not your logic that makes your partner feel safe.

It's your love.

Go Deeper With Theses Verses:

Isaiah 41:10, Proverbs 15:1, Romans 15:1–2, John 15:12

APPLICATION:

Use the CARE framework in one upcoming conversation:
- **C**onnect by listening without judgment
- **A**cknowledge their emotions (name them)
- **R**eassure with presence
- **E**ngage with follow-through

Reflect afterward:
- What went differently?
- What did your spouse need that they couldn't say directly?

Keep the CARE steps somewhere you'll see them. Practice using them when tension rises.

Pray This:

Jesus,

I want to be a safe place for my spouse, but sometimes I don't know how. I get defensive, distracted, or distant.

Help me to listen with compassion, respond with gentleness, and stay present in the moments that matter most.

Teach me to validate, not fix. To comfort, not control. To reflect Your care, even when I feel tired or frustrated.

Let our home be a place of emotional safety and spiritual healing.

In Your name, Amen.

8

WHEN LOVE FEELS ONE SIDED

THERE'S a particular ache that settles in when it feels like you're the only one trying. You initiate the conversations. You carry the emotional weight. You pursue connection. And your effort is met with indifference, or worse, silence. It's not the absence of love that hurts the most. It's the absence of response.

One-sided love doesn't always mean the other person doesn't care. Sometimes they're buried under their own shame, pain, or fear. But that doesn't make the ache any lighter. You still feel the imbalance. The quiet doubt creeping in: *How long can I keep doing this if nothing changes?*

Every marriage will hit uneven seasons, times when one person carries more. But when the imbalance becomes the norm... when effort is only coming from one side... it starts to feel like you're not just loving them, you're dragging the relationship behind you.

And it's exhausting.

You care. You're invested. You want connection. You've softened. You've prayed. You've apologized. But nothing changes. And slowly, something inside you starts to shut down. Not because you stopped loving them, but because you're tired of loving alone.

This chapter isn't here to offer quick fixes. It's here to name what often gets buried beneath performance, pressure, and pain: the slow ache of loving someone who won't meet you in it. And the quiet hope that even here, God sees. And He's not asking you to fix the relationship. He's inviting you to root yourself in the kind of love that never stops pursuing.

WHEN THE WEIGHT DOESN'T SHIFT

It usually starts small. One person is tired. The other is stressed. Life gets busy. But slowly, subtly, the pattern takes root: one spouse becomes the emotional lifeline of the relationship while the other drifts into silence.

You try. You bring up the hard conversations. You initiate affection, plan the date nights, carry the spiritual weight. You even adjust your tone, your timing, your words, hoping it will finally get through. But you're still met with detachment. Distance. A vague "I'm fine" while nothing changes.

Eventually, silence feels safer than hope.

You don't want to stop caring, but you're exhausted. You're not trying to be dramatic. You're just tired of being the only one who shows up.

That's when the deeper questions creep in:

- *Is this what marriage is supposed to feel like?*
- *Am I asking too much?*
- *Would they even notice if I stopped trying?*
- And worst of all...

- *Maybe I'm just too much. Maybe I am the problem.*

When love feels one-sided long enough, it doesn't just erode connection, it erodes identity. You stop asking for what you need because you've convinced yourself your needs are the issue. You start shrinking in your own story, afraid that your desire for intimacy will be mistaken for neediness. Or worse, ignored altogether.

But let's name this for what it is: chronic imbalance isn't sustainable. A marriage can survive a thousand stressors, but indifference is not one of them.

THE DRIFT: FROM PURSUER TO RESIGNED

In every relationship, there are moments when one person carries more weight than the other. But when those moments turn into months, and then into a quiet way of life, something begins to shift. The one who used to pursue starts to pull back. The one who once fought for connection begins to settle for coexistence.

It's not that you've stopped caring. You've just run out of ways to express it that don't end in disappointment. You've said the same things a hundred different ways. You've prayed. You've softened. You've waited. And yet, the gap remains.

What began as hope becomes heaviness. What started as desire becomes duty.

There's nothing wrong with wanting connection. You were made for it. But over time, the repeated effort without response begins to dull your spirit. You no longer expect change. You start avoiding the conversations that used to feel urgent. You learn to live with a low-grade ache, convincing yourself it's just part of marriage.

The drift doesn't happen all at once. It's the slow erosion of pursuit. The resignation that settles in when you've been met with too many blank stares or half-hearted nods. It's when you stop reaching, not because you don't care, but because you're protecting the little you have left.

And somewhere in the back of your mind, you wonder, how did we get here?

WHY IT HAPPENS: SHAME, FEAR, AND FALSE IDENTITY

When a spouse withdraws emotionally, it's easy to assume they simply don't care. But the truth is often more complicated. Emotional disconnection isn't always rooted in selfishness. It's frequently the byproduct of shame, fear, or a distorted sense of identity.

Some spouses don't shut down because they're indifferent, they shut down because they feel disqualified. Deep down, they carry the belief: *I'll never be enough, so why try?* Or they fear, *If I let you see all of me, you'll be disappointed.* So they hide. They keep things light. They give you the facts, but never their feelings.

Others over-function in the marriage, trying to do everything themselves. They've been shaped by the belief that if they stop performing, everything will fall apart. Their identity is so tied to being the "rescuer" or "fixer" that they don't know how to just be present without overcompensating.

In both cases, the relationship becomes lopsided. One person shuts down, and the other carries more than they were meant to. Over time, love starts to feel like labor. And instead of being a place of mutual connection, marriage starts to feel like a job only one person is clocking into.

But here's what's essential to remember: when your identity is rooted in Christ, you can stop striving to earn love or control outcomes. You don't love to become enough, you love because you already are.

THE WOUNDED PURSUER AND THE WITHHOLDING PROTECTOR

Many marriages settle into an unspoken pattern: one partner becomes the pursuer, the other the protector. One gets louder. One grows quieter. One pushes for closeness. The other pulls away to preserve peace.

The pursuer is often hurting but doesn't know how to say it without sounding demanding. So they try harder, ask more questions, express more disappointment. They long for reassurance and closeness, but their intensity starts to sound like criticism. What they want is connection. What it feels like to their spouse is pressure.

Meanwhile, the protector isn't trying to hurt anyone. They often believe their silence is safer. Their emotional withdrawal is an attempt to avoid conflict or failure. But what they don't realize is that silence itself becomes its own kind of wound. They might see themselves as staying calm or avoiding drama, but to their partner, it feels like abandonment.

Neither spouse wants to cause harm. But both are stuck in patterns that stem from fear, not identity. The pursuer is afraid of being alone. The protector is afraid of being inadequate. And as long as fear is leading, intimacy will always feel just out of reach.

Awareness is the first step toward change. When you can name the pattern, when you can say, "This is our dynamic, not our destiny," you give yourselves the chance to rewrite the script.

REFRAMING THE LIE: WHAT FEELS TRUE VS. WHAT IS TRUE

When love feels one-sided, the mind becomes fertile ground for lies. Silence starts to sound like a verdict. Disappointment whispers false narratives that take root before we even realize they've sprouted.

You start to believe:

- If I have to ask, it doesn't count.
- If they really loved me, I wouldn't need to say anything.
- If I stop trying, it'll all fall apart.
- God must be punishing me.
- I'm just too much, or not enough.

These thoughts don't just affect how you see your spouse, they begin to reshape how you see yourself. And over time, they train you to believe that your worth is tethered to someone else's response.

But here's the truth:

- It's not weakness to voice your needs. It's maturity.
- It's not wrong to set boundaries. It's stewardship.

- Your identity is not defined by someone else's effort.
- You are called to love, but not to control.
- You are called to be faithful, not to fix.

One-sided love will always tempt you to either strive harder or shut down completely. But there's a better way. Root your identity in who Christ says you are so you no longer have to react to your spouse's behavior, you can respond from your security in Him. You can love, not from desperation, but from overflow.

You don't need their perfect love to be whole. You already have a perfect Source.

THE MOST SECURE LOVE IS ROOTED IN SOMEONE BIGGER

One-sided love invites overreaction. You either try harder, hoping more effort will fix the disconnection, or you shut down to protect yourself from disappointment. But again, striving and silence are both rooted in fear. There's another way: to re-anchor your identity in the love of God.

The most secure love doesn't depend on your spouse's consistency. It depends on God's. Even the most faithful partner will fail sometimes. But God never will.

> *"Even to your old age and gray hairs I am he, I am he who will sustain you. I have made you and I will carry you; I will sustain you and I will rescue you."* — Isaiah 46:4

This kind of love doesn't deny reality, it redefines security. When you stop expecting your spouse to be your emotional source, you're free to love without fear of depletion. You don't love less; you just love differently. You love from wholeness, not from lack.

And that changes everything. You can set boundaries without bitterness. You can stay soft without losing strength. You can be faithful without forcing change. Because your anchor isn't their reaction, it's God's nature.

WHAT ONE-SIDED LOVE MIGHT SOUND LIKE

Emotional disconnection rarely begins with shouting matches. It surfaces in the slow erosion of ordinary conversations. The words may be simple, but underneath them is a story of longing, fear, and misinterpretation. Here's what those moments might sound like, and what's often really going on beneath the surface:

Wife: "I just don't feel like you even want to be around me anymore."
Translation: I miss you. I need to know I still matter.
Husband: "I'm here, aren't I?"
Translation: I don't know how to show up emotionally. Please don't ask for more.
Wife: "Being in the same room isn't the same as being with me."
Translation: I want connection, not just proximity.
Husband: "No matter what I do, it's never enough for you."
Translation: I feel like I'm failing, and I'm ashamed, so I'm turning it into blame.
Wife: "I just need to know we're in this together."

Translation: I'm not asking for perfect. I'm asking for presence.

These aren't just surface-level complaints, they're bids for connection. But when those bids aren't understood, both partners retreat. She's afraid of being abandoned. He's afraid of not measuring up. Both feel hurt. But neither knows how to break the cycle.

If you can learn to hear what's underneath the words, you can respond with empathy instead of defensiveness. And that shift, however small, is where reconnection begins.

FIVE ANCHORS FOR LOVING WITH CLARITY AND GRACE

It's tempting to default to survival strategies: over-functioning, withdrawing, blaming, or resigning. But there is a better way. These five anchors help reframe the path forward, not as a means to fix your spouse, but as a way to remain rooted in Christ, healthy in your identity, and wise in your love.

1. Pursue, Don't Perform

There's a difference between pursuing your spouse out of love and performing for them out of fear. Pursuit is intentional, grounded in strength. Performance is exhausting, driven by anxiety.

Ask yourself: *Am I loving to reflect who I am, or performing in hopes they'll finally respond?*

Pursuit makes space for grace. Performance chokes it.

2. Anchor Yourself in Identity First

You are not defined by how your spouse responds. You are defined by who God says you are: chosen, seen, beloved, secure. (Ephesians 1:4, Romans 8:38–39).

When you anchor your identity in Christ, you stop measuring your worth by someone else's emotional availability. You can love from overflow, not emptiness.

3. Set Boundaries Without Withdrawing Love

Boundaries are not the same as walls. A wall says, "Stay out." A boundary says, "Here's what's needed for love to thrive." Jesus modeled this. He loved fully, but He didn't enable dysfunction. He confronted, He clarified, and sometimes, He let people walk away.

You can say, "This isn't okay," without withdrawing your love. That's not cruelty, it's courage.

4. Shift from Scorekeeping to Stewardship

One of the quickest ways to poison love is to keep track of who's doing more. Love isn't a ledger, it's a gift. Scorekeeping leads to resentment. Stewardship leads to faithfulness.

Instead of asking, *Am I getting what I deserve?* Try asking, *Am I being who I'm called to be?*

You're not responsible for their effort. You are responsible for your heart.

5. Hold Room for God to Work

You are not the Holy Spirit. And that's a relief. Your job isn't to fix or convict, it's to remain faithful and rooted in love. Sometimes, God is working in unseen places. Sometimes, the seeds you've planted are growing slowly beneath the surface. Give God room to do what only He can do.

Release the outcome. Stay rooted in truth. Let grace do the slow work of restoration.

WHEN YOU'VE BEEN THE PASSIVE ONE

Not every one-sided dynamic begins with malice or neglect. Sometimes, it starts with silence, a hesitation, a missed moment, a subtle pulling back. Maybe you didn't know how to respond. Maybe you thought staying quiet was safer than saying the wrong thing. Maybe you convinced yourself your presence was enough.

But silence is never neutral. It creates space, and eventually that space starts to feel like distance.

If you've been emotionally absent or disengaged, the wake of that absence is felt. Your spouse may have stopped saying it out loud, but what they're really feeling is this: *"I miss you. I don't want to do this alone."*

You don't have to be perfect to re-engage. You just have to start showing up.

She's not asking for polished speeches or overnight change. She wants your heart, your real, imperfect, messy heart. She wants to know that you still care. That you're willing to try. That even if you don't have the right words, you're in this with her.

And if you're afraid of failing, afraid of not getting it right, that fear is exactly where grace wants to meet you.

Not to shame you, but to remind you: love is not about performance. It's about presence.

Don't underestimate what one moment of presence can restore. A look. A question. A hand reaching out. These are not small gestures, they're signals that say, *"I see you. I want to be close again. Let's find our way forward together."*

You don't need to have all the answers. You just need to take the first step.

LOVING LIKE JESUS—EVEN WHEN IT'S ONE-SIDED

There's a detail in the Gospels that wrecks me every time I stop and think about it. On the night Jesus was betrayed, He sat at the table with His closest friends, men He had lived with, served with, and led for years. He told them that one of them would betray Him.

And not one of them knew who it was.

Think about that.

Jesus had spent three years with Judas, knowing full well what Judas would eventually do. He knew the betrayal was coming. He saw the signs. And yet, He treated Judas with such consistent kindness, dignity, and grace that none of the disciples suspected a thing.

That kind of love doesn't come from insecurity or emotional desperation. It comes from identity.

Jesus didn't love Judas because Judas earned it. He loved because that's who Jesus is. His love wasn't reactive, it was rooted. It wasn't performative, it was secure. It wasn't based on Judas' behavior, it was based on the heart of the Father.

That's the kind of love we're called to reflect in our marriage.

I'm not saying you ignore betrayal or pretend brokenness doesn't exist. Jesus didn't do that either. But what He *did* model was a love that stayed steady even when it wasn't returned. A love that didn't withhold compassion as punishment. A love that didn't turn bitter, even when the pain was personal.

Imagine what your home would look like if you loved your spouse in a way that left no doubt, even in the hard seasons, that they were safe with you. Imagine if your presence carried the kind of consistency that made others wonder not "What will they do next?" but "How are they still showing up with peace?"

That's what love rooted in Christ can do. It doesn't excuse sin, but it also doesn't get infected by it. It stays grounded in identity. It chooses dignity over control. And when it's hard, it remembers: if Jesus could love Judas that well, we can love our spouse with grace, even when the story feels one-sided.

CLOSING CHARGE

One-sided love is one of the heaviest forms of love to carry. It takes more than willpower to keep showing up, it takes identity. It takes trust in a love that runs deeper than disappointment, stronger than silence, and more faithful than human effort.

If Jesus could love Judas with tenderness, you can love your spouse with grace. Not because they've earned it. But because that's who you are in Christ.

Don't lose yourself trying to fix them. But don't lose your heart trying to protect yourself, either. There's a better way.

Stay soft. Stay faithful. Stay anchored.

Because when you love from identity, not for validation, you reflect a God who never stops showing up.

Let this be the chapter that breathes permission into exhausted hearts. To speak truth. To set boundaries. To hold on. But most of all. to remember that your love is never really one-sided... not when you love from a source that never runs dry.

———

Go Deeper With These Verses:

Romans 5:8, Isaiah 46:4, Galatians 6:9, 1 Corinthians 13:7

———

APPLICATION:

If you feel like the only one trying in your marriage, pause and ask:

1. Am I loving from fullness or striving from emptiness?
2. What boundaries do I need to set, not to punish, but to protect what's good?
3. Where do I need to stop playing the role of the Holy Spirit in my spouse's life?

Write a prayer asking God to help you release the burden of fixing your marriage, and instead trust Him to work through your faithfulness.

RESET PROMPTS & PRACTICAL TOOLS

JOURNAL PROMPT:
What do I believe about my worth when my spouse doesn't respond the way I hope?
SAY IT BETTER SCRIPT:
"When I'm the only one trying, I start to believe I'm not

worth pursuing. I don't want to resent you, so I need to be honest: I'm feeling alone in this."

———

Pray This:

Father,

I feel like I'm the only one trying. Sometimes I wonder if love is even working.

But I know You see me. You don't waste faithful love.

Help me to stop trying to be the Holy Spirit in my marriage. Teach me to set boundaries with wisdom, not resentment. Let my love be fueled by You, not by fear or pressure.

Remind me that even if I feel alone, I am never abandoned.

In Jesus' name,

Amen.

9

HEALED BY LOVE, TRANSFORMED BY TRUTH

ONE OF THE most redemptive acts in marriage isn't fixing your spouse, it's reminding them who they are when they've forgotten. That's how Jesus loves us. He doesn't shame us into growth or scold us with disappointment. He simply says, *"You are Mine. You are loved. You are worth the cross."* That kind of love doesn't just correct, it heals.

But the wounds we carry into marriage don't always come from our spouse. Often, they come from years of believing lies about ourselves, lies like "I'm too broken," "I'll never be enough," or "I have to earn love to keep it."

When we believe those lies, they begin to share how we show up. We start acting out of insecurity. We react instead of respond. We shut down, overcompensate, or keep our guard up. And little by little, the story we believe about ourselves becomes the script we follow in our relationship.

The truth is, transformation doesn't start with trying harder. It starts with believing deeper. Identity isn't just a theological concept. It's the foundation for healing. You can't build a secure marriage if you're convinced you're unlovable. You can't reflect Christ when you think you're a failure. And you can't offer grace to your spouse if you haven't learned to receive it for yourself.

So how do we get unstuck? We confront the lies we've believed, and we replace them with truth.

THE VOICE WE CARRY

Every one of us carries an internal voice. Sometimes it echoes an old criticism. Sometimes it sounds like our own anxiety or self-doubt. Sometimes it disguises itself as self-awareness, but beneath it all, it repeats the same message: "You're not enough."

That voice affects everything. It shapes how you respond to your spouse. It influences whether you speak up or shut down. It determines how you handle conflict, receive affection, or offer forgiveness. And perhaps most dangerously, it can become so familiar that you stop questioning it.

But here's what I tell my clients all the time: Just because it's familiar doesn't mean it's true.

TEN LIES WE BELIEVE—AND THE TRUTH THAT SETS US FREE

Our culture loves phrases like "live your truth" or "speak your truth", as if truth is something we get to invent. But real healing doesn't come from repeating what feels true in the moment. It comes from returning to what *is* true, regardless of how we feel.

Because here's the reality: only the Creator has the authority to define the creation. If we don't root ourselves in God's truth, we'll keep building our identity on emotions, wounds, or past mistakes. And eventually, those shaky foundations will show up in our marriage.

This section isn't about shallow encouragement. It's about spiritual alignment. These ten lies are the ones I've seen most often in counseling, lies people carry into marriage that slowly choke out intimacy, security, and growth. But each one has a counter-voice from God. And it's that truth, not willpower, that rewrites the story.

Let's walk through them together.

#1: I tell myself, "I'm not good enough."

God's Truth: "You are fearfully and wonderfully made." (Psalm 139:14) You are a dwelling place of God (1 Cor. 3:16). You are born of God, and the evil one cannot touch you (1 John 5:18). I am a saint (Eph. 1:1; 1 Cor. 1:2; Phil. 1:1; Col. 1:2). You are not a mistake that marriage has to fix, you are a masterpiece learning how to love.

#2: I tell myself, "I'm a failure."

God's Truth: "I can do all things through Christ who strengthens me" (Philippians 4:13). Your past does not disqualify you. You are redeemed and forgiven. The record against you has been cancelled (Col. 1:14). The cross already declared you valuable and covered.

#3: I tell myself, "I'm inadequate."

God's Truth: "I am more than a conqueror through Christ" (Romans 8:37). You're not an imposter in your own marriage. You are a joint heir with Christ, complete in Him (Col. 2:10). In your weakness, His strength is made perfect. You are more than a conqueror (Romans 8:37).

#4: I tell myself, "I'm unlovable."

God's Truth: "I have loved you with an everlasting love." (Jeremiah 31:3) Even if your spouse struggles to show love, God's love for you never fluctuates. You were bought at a price. You are His, and He is not ashamed to call you His (1 Cor. 6:19-20).

#5: I tell myself, "I'm only as valuable as what I achieve."

God's Truth: "You are precious and honored in His sight" (Isaiah 43:4). Your value doesn't come from productivity. It comes from your position in Christ. You have been blessed with every spiritual blessing, not because of your resume, but because of your relationship (Eph. 1:3).

#6: I tell myself, "I'm alone in this."

God's Truth: "I will never leave you nor forsake you" (Hebrews 13:5). You are not carrying this marriage alone. Even if you feel unseen, you are not forgotten. God sees the weight you carry. You are a member of Christ's body, and you are never truly alone (1 Cor. 12:27).

#7: I tell myself, "I'm not as important as other people."

God's Truth: "You are the salt of the earth. You are the light of the world" (Matthew 5:13–14). Comparison is a thief. You are God's workmanship, created with purpose. You matter, not because of how visible you are, but because of how valuable you are to Him (Eph. 2:10).

#8: I tell myself, "I'm too broken to be used by God."

God's Truth: "You are a new creation in Christ" (2 Corinthians 5:17). God is not scared of your brokenness. In fact, He specializes in rebuilding what feels beyond repair. Your wounds are not the end of your story, they're the beginning of a testimony.

#9: I tell myself, "I'm weak if I show emotion."
God's Truth: "Jesus wept" (John 11:35). Emotion is not weakness. Jesus Himself expressed deep sorrow, compassion, and longing. You were created in the image of a God who feels. Don't let culture rob you of what God made holy.

#10: I tell myself, "I'm not worthy of respect."
God's Truth: "You are a royal priesthood, a holy nation, God's special possession" (1 Peter 2:9). Respect isn't earned by perfection. It flows from identity. You were created to walk with dignity, not because you've done everything right, but because He has made you righteous (Rom. 5:1).

You were never meant to fight your battles with half-truths and self-doubt. These promises aren't motivational slogans—they're declarations of who you are in Christ. They're the spiritual inheritance that rewrites your story from the inside out.

The more you internalize what God says about you, the less power the lies have. And the more you speak His truth, over your thoughts, over your marriage, over your wounds, the more you step into the freedom Jesus already secured for you.

You don't have to hustle to be enough. You already are, in Him.

HOW THESE LIES SHOW UP IN MARRIAGE

Knowing who you are in Christ is powerful, but it's not just about self-esteem. It's about how you show up in real relationships. Because the lies we believe don't stay tucked away in our thoughts, they shape our tone, our reactions, our decisions. And most of all, they shape how we relate to the person we've committed our life to.

When you believe you're not enough, you start trying to prove your worth. When you believe you're unlovable, you start building walls. When you believe you're alone, you stop asking for help. Here's what it often looks like behind closed doors, and what your marriage might need instead:

Lie #1: "I'm not good enough."

How it shows up: Perfectionism or people-pleasing.

You over-function. You manage every detail, run yourself ragged, and try to earn connection through performance. But when your efforts go unnoticed or unreciprocated, the disappointment cuts deep. Because underneath the striving is a fear: *If I'm not impressive, I won't be loved.*

What your marriage needs: Grace, not performance. You are not your to-do list. You are loved as you are, not as you accomplish.

Lie #2: "I'm a failure."

How it shows up: Defensiveness or shutdown.

You take every critique personally. Even gentle feedback feels like confirmation that you're falling short. You defend yourself, shut down, or withdraw, not out of pride, but out of shame. You're not trying to win the argument, you're trying to survive your own self-condemnation.

What your marriage needs: Humility that's anchored in identity. You can be wrong without being worthless. You can miss the mark without losing your value.

Lie #3: "I'm inadequate."

How it shows up: Controlling behavior or emotional distance.

You monitor, manage, and sometimes micromanage. Or you pull away before you get exposed. You compare yourself to your spouse's strengths. You wonder if they would be better off with someone else. Instead of intimacy, you choose image.

What your marriage needs: Vulnerability over control. Your worth isn't proven through performance, it's revealed through connection.

Lie #4: "I'm unlovable."

How it shows up: Withdrawing or testing your spouse.

You keep your heart at a distance or push your spouse away to see if they'll pursue. You brace for rejection, so you never give love a chance to land. If you've believed the lie long enough, you start sabotaging connection just to feel in control.

What your marriage needs: Reassurance through consistent presence, not just words. And a return to the truth that you are deeply, irrevocably loved by God.

Lie #5: "I'm only as valuable as what I achieve."

How it shows up: Workaholism or misplaced priorities.

You give your best energy to your career or public life, and your spouse gets the leftovers. You feel alive when you're achieving, but aimless when you're home. You don't mean to neglect the relationship, but it becomes background noise to your next accomplishment.

What your marriage needs: Rest. Reconnection. A recalibration of what really matters, and a reminder that your value isn't earned, it's received.

Lie #6: "I'm alone in this."

How it shows up: Resentment or martyrdom.

You carry the emotional labor, the parenting load, the household stress. You might not say it out loud, but you think, *If I don't do it, it won't get done.* Slowly, your helpfulness becomes exhaustion. Then bitterness. Then silent blame.

What your marriage needs: Vulnerable honesty, not silent endurance. You are not weak for asking for help. Your pain deserves to be named, not swallowed.

Lie #7: "I'm not as important as other people."

How it shows up: Self-silencing or passive resentment.

You stay quiet to keep the peace. You defer, accommodate, and put your needs last. But over time, the silence doesn't feel sacrificial, it feels suffocating. You start to feel invisible, not because your spouse doesn't care, but because you've convinced yourself you don't matter enough to speak.

What your marriage needs: Your voice. Your presence. Mutuality is not selfish, it's sacred.

Lie #8: "I'm too broken to be used by God."

How it shows up: Disengagement or spiritual apathy.

You feel like the weak link. You stop initiating prayer. You avoid vulnerability. You assume your brokenness makes you a burden. So instead of stepping forward in faith, you fade into the background.

What your marriage needs: A reminder that grace isn't for the perfect—it's for the willing. God doesn't sideline the broken. He empowers them.

Lie #9: "I'm weak if I show emotion."

How it shows up: Stoicism or emotional distance.

You're the steady one. The composed one. But that steadiness starts to feel like absence. You don't cry. You don't open up. And while you may think you're protecting your spouse from your emotions, what they feel is disconnection.

What your marriage needs: Emotional presence. Honesty. The courage to let your spouse into the places you usually keep guarded.

Lie #10: "I'm not worthy of respect."

How it shows up: Passivity or self-deprecation.

You stop leading. You stop offering input. You don't believe your thoughts or presence carry much weight, so you downplay your voice. And over time, your spouse stops hearing it, not out of disrespect, but because you stopped speaking up.

What your marriage needs: Confidence rooted in Christ. You were created to stand, not because you demand honor, but because you were already declared worthy by the One who made you.

PULLING IT TOGETHER

Every one of these lies, if left unchallenged, becomes a silent architect in your marriage. They don't just sit in your head —they script your story. They influence your tone, your trust, your timing. They erode confidence and reinforce fear.

But here's the truth: You don't have to live by lies.

You don't have to let shame dictate your identity. You don't have to let fear filter your reactions. You don't have to stay stuck in patterns that were built around self-protection instead of love.

Because the moment you start recognizing the lie, naming it, and replacing it with truth, something shifts. You begin to relate from identity instead of insecurity. You begin to respond with grace instead of fear. You start building a marriage that reflects God's voice instead of the inner critic.

That's when love becomes healing. But the danger of lies isn't just that they hurt, it's that they distort what we see. They become lenses. You don't just hear "You're not enough", you start *seeing* rejection in every silence. You don't just hear "You're too much", you start *feeling* like a burden even when your spouse is trying to connect. You don't just hear "You'll never change", you start *acting* like transformation isn't possible.

I've seen it countless times in counseling. One spouse tries to love the other, but their love keeps hitting a wall of insecurity. They say, "You matter to me," but it's met with skepticism. They offer forgiveness, but it's dismissed. It's not that the love isn't real. It's that the lie has been louder than the truth.

That's why healing doesn't begin with fixing behavior, it begins with replacing false identity.

WHAT HEALING ACTUALLY LOOKS LIKE

It Begins with Identity

Healing in marriage isn't just about stopping the yelling or learning better timing. It's about putting down roots in something deeper, something immovable.

At its core, healing begins with identity. Not with better strategies. Not with behavior modification. Not even with forgiveness, though that matters. It begins with replacing the lies that have shaped you with the truth of who God says you are.

I will continue to reiterate that you can't love well if you believe you're unlovable. You can't receive love if you think you're a burden. You can't lead well if you're convinced you're a failure.

So much of the pain we see in marriage is downstream from a broken view of self. We don't just react to our spouse, we react to the story we're carrying inside. A spouse who lashes out may not be cruel; they're afraid they're not enough. A spouse who withdraws isn't always distant; they might be convinced they're not worth pursuing.

That's why surface-level change doesn't last. You can't build healthy connection on top of a cracked identity. It's like building a house on sand.

Clinical Insight: Identity-Based Behavior

In emotionally focused therapy (EFT), we often say: "The issue isn't the issue, the issue is the meaning underneath."

When a spouse says, "You never listen," what they often mean is, "I don't feel important." When someone slams the door or walks away, it's not always defiance, it might be shame trying to escape. Underneath the argument about parenting is a belief: *"I'm not doing enough."* Underneath the silence is a question: *"Do I even matter to you?"*

These core beliefs don't originate in marriage, they get activated in marriage. And until we confront them, we'll keep reacting from them. This is where theology and therapy meet: true healing starts when we let God's truth reframe our identity. Romans 12:2 calls it the renewing of our minds. John 8:32 says that truth sets us free, not performance, not pressure, but truth.

God's Word doesn't just tell us what to do, it tells us who we are. And once you begin living from that place, everything starts to shift.

Healing Is Modeled, Not Demanded

When marriage feels stuck, our default is to correct. We explain. We persuade. We push harder. And when that doesn't work, we double down, believing the right logic or strong enough delivery will finally break through. But healing doesn't happen through pressure. It happens through presence. Healing isn't something you force, it's something you reflect.

The most powerful changes I've seen in marriages didn't come from lectures. They came from one spouse choosing to live from identity even when the other didn't. They chose consistency over control. Grace over guilt. Security over shame. And in doing so, they didn't just speak truth, they embodied it.

This is what Jesus did. He didn't pressure people into change. He loved them in a way that made change possible. He didn't berate Peter for failing, He re-commissioned him. He didn't shame the woman at the well, He restored her dignity. Jesus didn't rush transformation. He invited it. That's the difference between control and Christlike influence.

You don't need to preach to your spouse to bring healing. You need to live it. You need to respond differently. Speak more gently. Stay rooted when they're reactive. Set boundaries without bitterness. Own your voice without losing your love.

And even if they don't change right away, even if they never fully respond, you'll know you didn't lose your own character trying to chase theirs.

You may not be able to force healing. But you can model it. And that's often the spark that opens the door for God to move.

WHAT SPEAKING IDENTITY LOOKS LIKE IN MARRIAGE

When your spouse is acting out of insecurity, frustration, or fear, it's easy to react. To take it personally. To
match their mood. But most of the time, the reason
they're out of sync with you is because they're out of
sync with themselves. They've lost sight of who
they are.

That's when love becomes something more than a feeling. It becomes a reminder. Instead of saying, "You need to
get it together," identity-based love says, "This isn't who
you are." Instead of trying to fix their behavior, it reflects
back who they were created to be. Not in a patronizing way.
Not in a moment of pride. But with quiet strength rooted in
truth.

It sounds like:

- "You're not defined by this mistake."
- "You're worth loving, even on your worst day."
- "You're still the person I chose. And God hasn't
  changed His mind about you."

This isn't blind optimism. It's spiritual clarity.

Because when someone forgets who they are, and they
are lost in the woods of their false identity, they need a
compass. And you can't force them to believe it, but you can
hand them the map. You can name the truth even when
shame is loud. You can hold the line of grace when they're
spiraling in guilt. You can help them remember what God
says, even when they're too discouraged to hear it for
themselves.

And when you do that consistently, not as a performance, but from a place of identity, it becomes the clearest picture of Christ your spouse might ever see.

———

There was one couple I worked with where the husband had been unfaithful. The betrayal was deep. The pain was real. The trust was shattered.

And yet, the wife, though heartbroken, made a decision early on that stunned me.

She said, "I'm not going to pretend this didn't hurt. And I'm not going to act like nothing needs to change. But I also know this: you are not your worst decisions."

She said it with a supernatural sense of strength and confidence. Again and again, when shame would rise in him, she'd say, "That's not who you are anymore." When he started to spiral, she'd say, "You're not a failure, you're my husband. And I see who you truly are."

When he doubted whether he was even worth rebuilding with, she reminded him, "God's not done with us. And I'm not done either." She wasn't excusing what happened. She was fighting for his identity.

And it changed everything. Sure, there were times when they struggled and times when he would fall into traps of defensiveness and self-preservation. But she was consistent in extending grace through his growing pains.

That type of love broke him, in the best way. When I first met with him, he listed his identity as: "I'm a cheater, borderline evil, destructive, and selfish." (said through a filter of shame and guilt) But as we worked through his shame and the lies he'd believed, and as his wife kept showing up with grace, something shifted.

He began to say things like: "I'm forgiven. I'm loved. I'm whole. I'm learning to be the man I forgot I was."

He realized that the more destructive he'd been, the further he had drifted from his true identity. But it was her grace, undeserved and unwavering, that helped him find the way back. Her love reminded him of who he was before the sin. Before the failure. Before the lies.

And that reminder became louder than the voice of shame. Over time, he began to show up differently. He owned his mistakes. He pursued her heart. He rebuilt trust with humility instead of fear. Not because she demanded it, but because she loved him in a way that called him home. The love she offered him didn't come out of response to him changing and being more faithful or reliable, it came from her confidence in her identity in Christ and led to his change and his faithfulness. She loved first and the change naturally followed.

That's the kind of love that heals. It doesn't just name the wound, it names the truth. It doesn't say, "Be better." It says, "You already belong, now live like it."

CLOSING CHARGE

Picture this: your spouse walks into the room carrying the emotional weight of shame, insecurity, or failure. It's not visible, but it clings to them like mud. Every word, every reaction, is touched by it. And it's messy. It gets on you. It affects the atmosphere. The tension rises.

Your instinct may be to clean it up. To fix it. To scold. To get them to see what they're doing and how it's affecting you. But here's the hard truth: you're not the Holy Spirit. And trying to be Him only deepens the disconnection.

But there is something you *can* be: His echo.

You can reflect the same voice God uses with you. A voice that speaks truth, not accusation. Grace, not guilt. Identity, not insecurity. You can love your spouse in a way that reminds them of who they are, even when they've forgotten. Not because you're excusing their pain, but because you're choosing to be a mirror of Christ's presence in it.

That kind of love doesn't mean silence. It doesn't mean tolerating abuse or pretending things are okay when they're not. It means holding your boundaries while keeping your heart soft. It means staying rooted in your identity, not your spouse's response. It means speaking to their spirit, not just their behavior.

So here's the challenge:

- When your spouse withdraws in shame, you don't have to chase them, but you *can* stay steady.
- When insecurity flares, you don't have to escalate, but you *can* speak peace.
- When they forget who they are, you don't have to fix them, but you *can* remind them.

You won't always get it right. Neither will they. But love that reflects the Holy Spirit, kind, clear, consistent, is what softens the heart and reshapes the story.

You are not your spouse's Holy Spirit. But you are God's chosen voice of grace in their life. And that voice can echo louder than shame when you choose to speak identity, not just correction. In a culture of pressure and performance, that kind of love is revolutionary.

Go Deeper With These Verses

John 8:32, 2 Corinthians 5:17, Romans 8:1, James 5:16

APPLICATION:

Identify one lie your spouse believes about themselves.

(You may have heard them say it out loud: "I'm never enough." "I ruin everything.")

Ask yourself:

• Do I reinforce that lie, or speak against it?

• What would it sound like to speak truth to their identity instead of reacting to their behavior?

Choose one moment this week to affirm your spouse's identity, out loud. Not because they earned it. But because it's who God says they are.

———

Pray This:

Jesus,

There are lies I've believed for far too long, about myself, about my spouse, about our story.

But You are truth. And You are love. And Your love heals what truth reveals. Help me to replace shame with grace, bitterness with forgiveness, fear with faith. Teach me to speak identity over my spouse, not because they always act lovable, but because they are deeply loved by You. Let our marriage be a place of healing, not hiding. Of restoration, not resentment.

In Your name, Amen.

EPILOGUE

EDEN WASN'T JUST A PLACE, it was the original stage where our identity and Truth walked hand in hand. Intimacy with God. Vulnerability without shame. Purpose that flowed from identity.

That's what we lost in the Fall. But it's also what Christ came to restore.

Marriage isn't a detour from God's design, it's a stage for it. A covenant that invites you to become more, not by trying harder, but by returning to the truth of who you are and Whose you are. Every fight, every wound, every moment of misunderstanding is a chance, not just to get it right, but to get real. To be known. To choose love again.

You will fail. You will forget. You'll drift from who you were created to be. But you don't have to stay lost. Because love still comes looking. Just like it did in the garden.

Just like it did on the cross.

This isn't about going back to Eden. It's about echoing it, living in a way that reflects what was lost, and what can be found again. The closer you get to Jesus, the more Jesus comes out of you. That's why this book doesn't end with a list of tools or tips, it ends with an invitation: to know Him deeper. Because ultimately, the restoration of your identity and marriage doesn't depend on better strategies, it depends on the One who made you. You don't need more hacks or more hustle. You need Jesus. And He's ready to meet you in the in-between.

You were made for this love.

A love that sees. A love that stays. A love that surrenders. You don't have to earn your way back to who you were made to be. The resurrection already cleared the path. Because Jesus rose, your identity is no longer up for grabs. It's secured, sealed, and spoken for. And the same power that rolled away the stone can roll away your shame, and remind you who you are.

A FINAL STORY: MY BROTHER'S BATTLE WITH IDENTITY

As I finish this book, I keep thinking about my brother, Kyle. His story is never far from my mind. In so many ways, he lived out the themes of this book, sometimes in the light, but often in the shadows.

Kyle was incredibly intelligent. He could talk circles around anyone, wielding logic like a shield. But beneath the wit and sarcasm was a man who never fully believed he was enough. He wore his intellect like armor. It was how he protected himself from the vulnerability he didn't know how to carry.

His drinking began in high school. That's when his internal struggle started to become visible. He was a perfectionist, hard on himself and driven to meet impossible standards. After a DUI in high school, it was like something broke in him. I don't think he ever truly forgave himself. He believed that one mistake ruined everything. And no matter how hard he tried to move forward, shame clung to him like a shadow.

He drank in secret, hiding bottles in drawers, closets, and toilets. He hated that part of himself, but he didn't know how to live without it. Eventually, he hit a breaking point and tried to rob a liquor store for two bottles of vodka. That moment landed him in jail, but even that wasn't the lowest point. Because for Kyle, the real prison was internal. He was caught in a cycle of shame and striving, always trying to prove he was okay while secretly believing he wasn't.

Our family lived in that tension for years. Holidays were layered with anxiety, not knowing which version of Kyle would show up. And while there were hospital visits and rehab stints and hard conversations, there were also moments, quiet glimpses, that reminded us God wasn't done with him. He dreamed of building a lifestyle company. He had a landscaping business. He excelled at golf. He had talent, ambition, and a heart that still longed for something more. But I don't think he trusted that God was with him. He thought he had to prove his worth before he could receive love. And that belief kept him locked in a cycle of striving and shame.

My relationship with Kyle was complicated. I loved him, and I truly believe he loved me too. But in recent years, there was a tension between us, like he wanted me to be happy but resented me for having what he couldn't find for himself. There were unspoken things between us, hurts we both carried. But even in that, we never stopped talking. We never stopped hoping there was more for us.

The week leading up to his death was one of the most

heartbreaking and healing weeks of my life. He was in a coma, and I spent nearly every day at his bedside. I prayed. I talked to him. I apologized for my part in our conflict. I forgave him for his. I remembered with him, even if he couldn't respond. There was something sacred in those days, like God was doing work in both of us, peeling back layers we had built over years of misunderstanding.

Kyle's body had finally begun to reflect the damage of the internal war he had been fighting for years. He was in complete organ failure, his liver, kidneys, and lungs were shutting down. Machines were doing what his body could no longer manage on its own. Every update from the doctors felt heavier than the last. And yet, in the middle of all that, we still held onto a fragile hope. Not that he would be physically healed, but that somehow, in his final days, he might finally know peace.

That week felt like God was turning off every other voice in Kyle's head, shutting down the noise of shame and lies, so that the truth could finally get through. So that love could finally be heard. I believe God was preparing Kyle's heart, softening the edges of his pain, dismantling the false identities he'd clung to for so long.

And then, on Friday, the day before he passed, God did the impossible.

Kyle woke up.

The doctors said it wasn't possible. In fact they had told us the plan was to remove him from the ventilator because there was no chance he will wake up again. They had already prepared us for the worst. But for ten sacred minutes, Kyle was awake, fully present. My sister, my parents, and I were all in the room. He looked at us, and for the first time in years, we saw something in his eyes that we hadn't seen in over a decade: peace. Not forced, not faked, real, deep, undeniable peace. It was like the striving had stopped. The walls had fallen. The love had finally landed.

That ten-minute miracle will stay with me for the rest of my life. It was God's way of saying, *I never gave up on him. And I never will.*

I share this because some of you might feel like it's too late. Like you've wandered too far, tried too long, or failed too many times to find your way back. But if there's one thing I've learned from Kyle's story, it's this: it is never too late to come home to who you truly are in Christ.

Even if your life feels like a tangle of false starts, failed attempts, and broken dreams, God's invitation to identity doesn't expire. His love is steady, even in the final hour. And the same grace that met Kyle in his last breath is the grace that meets you today.

You don't have to fix yourself first. You don't have to pretend anymore. You just have to stop running, let go of the lies, and let Him lead you back to who you were always meant to be.

QUESTIONS YOU MAY HAVE
ASKED WHILE READING

1. What does it mean to be fearfully and wonderfully made?

The statement "I am fearfully and wonderfully made" comes from Psalm 139:14. It's often quoted to suggest that I, in my present human form, have been made perfectly by God. But actually, verse 14 might not refer to us. The language of "fearful and wonderful" appears in the Psalm in reference to God: God's thoughts are "too wonderful" for me to comprehend (v. 6), and God's works are "wonderful" (v. 14). So Psalm 139:14 most likely reads, "I will praise you, for YOU are fearful and wonderful."

But the *next* parts of the psalm describe the ways that God has fashioned us. And the focus of the entire psalm is that God *knows* us. He's intimately acquainted with us (vv. 1-6). There's no place I can go in this universe that God won't find me there (vv. 7-12). He *knows* me because he *created* me (vv. 13-16). And because he created me, he *cares* for me (vv. 17-24). So maybe the psalm doesn't say that I'm perfect the way I am just because God made me. Let's be honest: what God makes we tend to ruin. But it *does* say that He made me, that he cares for me, and will walk me through hard times to become the person He created me to become.

2. What does it mean to be made a new creation?

Paul wrote, "If anyone is in Christ he is a new creation; old things have gone away, new things have come" (2 Corinthians 5:17). The hope and promise of life in Christ is that we are not bound to those old things we have become. What does all that mean?

We ruined God's first attempt at creation. God made everything there is, and the refrain in Genesis 1 is "and it was good." But when we get to Gen. 3 we find humanity rebelling against God, ruining their relationship with him, and corrupting the Garden of Eden. Ever since then, God has been trying to redeem this whole situation, and the key to it is the arrival, work, and ministry of Jesus. That's why so much of the NT is couched in terms of a "new creation" that God is doing in Christ. Jesus is the "new Adam" (Rom. 5:12-21; cf. 1 Cor. 15:22), the faithful man God has been looking for. Jesus crushes the head of the serpent (the one that deceived Adam and Eve) at the cross and in his resurrection (Gen. 3:15). And John describes the heavenly existence in Revelation 21-22 as a return to Eden.

So what does Paul mean when he says we are a "new creation?" It means that God has redeemed us and put us back on the path that he intended for us. It doesn't mean that the consequences of my sin magically disappear. It means those sins are not held against me in the eyes of God. If you are in Christ, that new path has been laid out for you. And you're no longer bound to make the same mistakes that put you in sin. Because of Jesus, everything is in the process of becoming "new."

3. What is the difference between Validation and Agreement?

Validation is acknowledging someone's internal experience, what they feel, think or perceive. Think Acceptance.

Agreement is about aligning yourself with their interpretation of what is true or right. It's being on the same page logically. Validation is being on the same page emotionally. Validation meets the heart's need to be seen. Agreement speaks to the mind's need to be right.

You can validate without agreement. You can say, "I understand that felt unfair," without saying, "You're right, I was unfair." Validation says, "I see how this made sense to you in that moment." Agreement says, "I share your conclusion."

4. So am I supposed to just ignore my spouse's mistakes?

No, grace is not the same thing as passivity. Forgiveness doesn't mean blindness. Ignoring your spouse's mistakes doesn't heal the relationship, it just buries the wound. True grace doesn't pretend nothing happened; it simply refuses to let what happened become the lens through how you see your spouse.

So don't ignore your spouse's mistakes, but don't magnify them either. Bring them to the light, gently. Lead with grace. Ephesians 4:15 says, "Speak truth in love, growing in every way more and more like Christ." This doesn't just mean speaking truth to help your spouse be more like Christ. It means speak truth and you will grow to be more like Christ in the way you extend that grace.

5. What is the difference between humility and insecurity?

At first glance, humility and insecurity can look similar. Both can appear soft-spoken, deferential, even self-effacing. But they come from very different roots.

Insecurity is self-preoccupation; humility is self-awareness.

Insecurity says, "I'm not enough." It's an identity issue, a heart turned inward, constantly measuring worth, replaying failure, and seeking validation. Insecurity keeps you trapped in the question of whether you matter. It shrinks you.

Humility, on the other hand, says, "Even in my lacking, God is enough...and therefore with Christ I am enough." It's an identity anchored in truth, a heart turned upward, resting in grace. Humility doesn't devalue you; it rightly values God and therefore, sees yourself and others clearly.

6. What if I feel like my spouse is attacking my identity in conflict?

The reality is that every time we are in conflict it is because something has brushed up near our false identity and insecurities. Sometimes things crash directly into them. Words hit hard when they collide with a would you already believe about yourself.

But here's the truth: your spouse doesn't have the power to name you. Only God does. When you anchor your identity in Him, you can stay grounded even when emotions flare. That doesn't mean you ignore hurtful words, it means you don't let them rewrite your worth and distract you into unhealthy reactions. You are who God says you are. And that truth leads you to Colossians 3:15, "Let the peace of Christ rule in your hearts."

7. Can God still use a broken marriage?

Absolutely. In fact, that's where His glory often shines the brightest. God doesn't waste pain, He redeems it. A broken marriage becomes sacred ground when both spouses surrender their pride, confess their sin, and allow grace to rebuild what self once tore down. The cracks in the relationship don't disqualify you from God's purpose; they become the very places where His mercy seeps through. Scripture is full of stories where human failure became the backdrop for divine restoration. A marriage doesn't have to be perfect to be powerful—it just has to be surrendered.

8. What is the difference between being made in God's image and being conformed to Christ's image (Romans 8:29)?

Being *made in God's image* speaks to creation; being *conformed to Christ's image* speaks to redemption. Every human bears the imprint of God's likeness, His capacity for relationship, creativity, reason, and love. That's what Genesis describes. But sin distorted that image, leaving us fractured and self-focused.

To be *conformed to the image of Christ* is the process of restoration, God shaping us back into who we were meant to be through the life of His Son. It's not about becoming divine; it's about reflecting the divine nature through our character. Where the image of God gives us identity, being conformed to Christ gives us transformation. The first shows what we were created to be; the second shows what grace can make us again.

NOTES & BIBLIOGRAPHY

Scripture quotations throughout this book are taken from the **English Standard Version (ESV)**, unless otherwise noted.

Black, Jeremy. *The War of Jenkins' Ear: The Forgotten Struggle for North and South America: 1739–1748*. Stackpole Books, 1990.
Encyclopædia Britannica Online, "War of Jenkins' Ear."

Carter, C. S. (1998). Neuroendocrine perspectives on social attachment and love. *Psychoneuroendocrinology, 23*(8), 779–818.

Collins, R. (2009). The teleological argument: An exploration of the fine-tuning of the universe. In W. L. Craig & J. P. Moreland (Eds.), *The Blackwell Companion to Natural Theology* (pp. 202–281). Oxford: Wiley-Blackwell.

Feldman, R. (2012). Oxytocin and social affiliation in humans. *Hormones and Behavior, 61*(3), 380–391.

Frey, W. H. (1985). *Crying: The Mystery of Tears*. Minneapolis: Winston Press.

Hamilton, V. P. (1990). *The Book of Genesis, Chapters 1–17*. Grand Rapids: Eerdmans.

Johnson, S. (2013). *Love sense: The revolutionary new science of romantic relationships*. Little, Brown and Company.

Kober, H., Buhle, J., Weber, J., Ochsner, K. N., & Wager, T. D. (2017). Letting go: Prayer and the self-regulation of brain activity. *Social Cognitive and Affective Neuroscience, 12*(5), 755–761.

Lazar, S. W., Kerr, C. E., Wasserman, R. H., Gray, J. R., Greve, D. N., Treadway, M. T., ... & Fischl, B. (2005). Meditation experience is associated with increased cortical thickness. *NeuroReport, 16*(17), 1893–1897.

Lloyd-Jones, Martyn. Spiritual Depression: Its Causes and Cure. Grand Rapids, MI: Eerdmans, 1965.

Moody, Dwight L. *An Address at Cambridge University*, 1883. Reprinted in *The Life of Dwight L. Moody* by William R. Moody. New York: Revell, 1900.

Plutarch. *Life of Theseus*, 23.1. Translated by Bernadotte Perrin. Cambridge, MA: Harvard University Press, 1914.

Rees, M. (1999). *Just Six Numbers: The Deep Forces that Shape the Universe*. New York: Basic Books.

Sarna, N. M. (1989). *Genesis: The Traditional Hebrew Text with the New JPS Translation*. Philadelphia: Jewish Publication Society.

Vingerhoets, A. J. J. M. (2013). *Why Only Humans Weep: Unravelling the Mysteries of Tears*. Oxford: Oxford University Press.

The reflections and practical insights shared here are drawn from a blend of personal experience, professional counseling practice, and biblical principles. Any client stories are shared with permission or have been carefully anonymized to protect privacy.

ACKNOWLEDGMENTS

I couldn't have written this book without the faithful love and partnership of my wife, Kristen. You have walked beside me in every step of this journey, your strength, your insight, and your unwavering faith have anchored me.

Thank you to my clients, who have trusted me with their stories and taught me what it means to show up with compassion.

And to everyone who has carried me in prayer, believed in this message, and encouraged me along the way, this book is as much yours as it is mine.

Thank you to Dr. Les Hardin, Professor of New Testament at Kentucky Christian University for your support, guidance, feedback and meaningful words shared in the Foreword.

Thank you to Brent, Dave, and Wes and all of those who helped launch this book to a success.

ABOUT THE AUTHOR

Tyler Olsen is a licensed mental health counselor and marriage therapist, known for weaving together practical insight and gospel-centered identity work. He has worked with countless couples navigating the gap between insecurity and intimacy, and he writes with the same honesty he brings to his counseling room. He lives in Jacksonville, FL with his wife, Kristen, and their two children.

You can find more of his work or potentially book a session with Tyler at his website, TylerOlsenTherapy.com

You can also find him on Social Media:

@TylerOlsenTherapy

Made in the USA
Middletown, DE
24 November 2025

22267893R00116